Count *on* Me

Count *on* Me

Tales of
Sisterhoods and
Fierce Friendships

Las Comadres Para Las Americas
Edited by Adriana V. López

ATRIA PAPERBACK

New York London Toronto Sydney New Delhi

ATRIA PAPERBACK

A Division of Simon & Schuster, Inc.
1230 Avenue of the Americas
New York, NY 10020

First Atria Paperback edition September 2012

ATRIA PAPERBACK and colophon are trademarks of Simon & Schuster, Inc.

For information about special discounts for bulk purchases, please contact Simon & Schuster Special Sales at 1-866-506-1949 or business@simonandschuster.com.

The Simon & Schuster Speakers Bureau can bring authors to your live event. For more information or to book an event, contact the Simon & Schuster Speakers Bureau at 1-866-248-3049 or visit our website at www.simonspeakers.com.

Designed by Jill Putorti

Manufactured in the United States of America

10   9   8   7   6   5   4   3   2   1

Count on me : tales of sisterhoods and fierce friendships / by Las Comadres Para Las Americas.—1st Atria Books trade pbk. ed.
  p. cm.
1. Hispanic American women—Biography. 2. Hispanic American women—Social life and customs. 3. Hispanic American women—Social conditions. 4. Female friendship—United States. 5. Female friendship—America. 6. Social networks—United States. 7. Social networks—America. 8. Las Comadres Para Las Americas. I. Las Comadres Para Las Americas.
E184.S75C68 2012
177'.62082—dc23   2012015552

ISBN: 978-1-4516-4201-8
ISBN: 978-1-4516-6296-2 (ebook)

*For my husband, Jack Bell, who has made the success
of Las Comadres Para Las Americas possible through
his unstinting support.*

*To my mothers: Sofia Flores de Hoyos, who molded me,
and Enriqueta Flores De La Garza, who gave me life.*

*To my twins, Paul and Ariel Comstock,
who inspire me every day.*

CONTENTS

INTRODUCTION

There is no question that women's relationships are unique, and so is the organization we named Las Comadres Para Las Americas®. A landmark UCLA study found that reaching out to friends is a woman's natural response to stress. It is said these friendships can bring us peace, fill the emotional shortcomings in our romantic relationships, and help us remember what lies deep inside every one of us. Women are a source of strength to each other. And despite our busy schedules, we as women need to have a relaxed space in which we can do the special kind of soul-searching talk we do when we gather with other women. Without it, we weaken.

Las Comadres Para Las Americas helps provide that time and space for women, but another reason why the organization resonates with thousands of Latinas is the familiar Spanish-language term in our name: *comadres*. The term encompasses some of the most complex and important relationships that exist between women. Comadres are best friends, confidants, coworkers, advisors, neighbors, and godmothers to one's children. The term is also used to describe midwives, and there may be no more intimate a moment than one woman helping another bring a child into the world. Comadre is indeed a powerful term, and concept, and its connotations are unique to Latino culture. All Latinas recognize the most common definition of the term comadre—the one related to friendship and camaraderie. Comadres are the women they know they can count on, lean on, and ask for advice or for help when needed. Like Las Comadres Para Las Americas, comadres make up the support system women create for themselves on the personal and professional fronts.

Comadres acquire a particular level of importance for Latinas living in an Anglo world—in addition to serving as a source of comfort, understanding, and inspiration, these women also serve as direct links to their cultural and family heritage. Sometimes, when a woman's family is far away or is a cause of strain on her daily life, comadres become a surrogate family that doesn't hold judgment. Comadre-type friendships can also blossom with non-Latinos who appreciate a Latina's openness and warmth in her manner of showing affection.

Aside from finding a comadre to enrich your life, I believe another important piece to the puzzle comes from reading books by Latino authors. A journey through a writer's words and similar experiences can provide the ultimate connection to another human being. This anthology was a dream Esmeralda Santiago and I talked about several years ago. She has been the spokesperson for the book club that forms part of Las Comadres Para Las Americas and I cherish her friendship from the bottom of my heart. The idea of bringing together a sampling of Latino literature's most vibrant voices on the topic of female friendships seemed the natural next step. But without the book club,

there might have never been an anthology. And I find it important to explain why it occurred to me to begin a book club in the
first place. Emblazoned in my memory is a specific experience
that led me down this path: A young Latina in her midtwenties,
who had recently graduated from college, was volunteering in
my office. Since I had no funds to pay her, I gave her a book
by an author who also happened to be a comadre. She looked
at it and said, "I have never read a Latina writer before." I was
stunned. Then I realized that this had been my own experience
not so long before, and that I needed to help to change that.
When the next uninitiated Latina walks through my door, I will
hand her this anthology in hopes of inspiring her.

   This collection of stories by prominent Latino authors is a
table spread out with snapshots of friendships that overcame
their difficult moments, but survived because of the humor and
humanity comadres can offer, even in the darkest moments. A
comadre or the idealized notion of comadreship can also mani-
fest itself in various ways throughout a woman's life. In "Las
Comais," Esmeralda Santiago recounts her mother's close-knit
relationships with a small and colorful army of comadres in
1950s Puerto Rico, which became an inspiration for Santiago in
both her creative and personal life. In "Every Day of Her Life,"
Carolina De Robertis takes on the role of caretaker for her de-
ceased friend's unpublished first novel, as if it were her beloved
comadre's child, her flesh and blood. If life is a highway, Stephanie Elizondo Griest sets out in "Road Sisters" on a journey with
an unfamiliar copilot whose eventual friendship winds up steering her away from life's dead ends, and back on the right path.

   In "Crocodiles and Plovers," Lorraine López remembers

how a prominent yet reticent alpha author on campus guided her through the rough waters of academia, and how López figured out a way to give back to her mentor in her own fashion. In Latin America, politics or corruption can either separate two women or bring them together for a cause. Fabiola Santiago's "Letters from Cuba" describes a tender childhood friendship that withstood the test of time, revolution, and lost correspondences. In "Casa Amiga: In Memory of Esther Chávez Cano," Teresa Rodríguez pays a moving tribute to a woman who gave her life to defend women from the violence in Juárez, Mexico, while finding the time to be a comadre to thousands.

Long-lasting and deep friendships can be formed quickly, and sometimes in the most unexpected moments or places. When two artists with different creative styles meet at a New York City event in Sofia Quintero's "The Miranda Manual," neither would have expected that they would end up sharing their personal and celluloid dreams together, as well as be committed to each other through sickness and health. In "My Teacher, My Friend," Reyna Grande relives the hardships she underwent, after emigrating from Mexico only to reconnect with an abusive father, until she walked into a classroom and met the woman who would inspire her to become a writer. In "Cooking Lessons," chef extraordinaire Daisy Martínez recounts the day she invited three young fans, whom she met on social networking sites, to her home to create an exquisite meal that they would all savor for a lifetime.

Comadres can save your life, and they can be as wild and risk-taking as Thelma and Louise, who without each other might not have been able to walk away from an abusive relationship and unhappy home life. In "Anarchy Chicks," Michelle Herrera Mulligan finds herself a rebellious friend at school whose fearlessness helps them plow through the pains of adolescence, dysfunctional families, and racial differences. The fact is, female friendships are scientifically proven to be good for one's health, and in her essay "A Heart-to-Heart Connection," Dr. Ana Nogales not only discusses why strong social support networks help prevent depression in women, but shares her own struggles with both fitting in and finding true comadres throughout her life. In Nogales's words, "When we join with other women and learn that our experiences are similar to those of our comadres, we create a sacred space in which to heal." The final story in this collection proves that not only women can be honorary comadres, but so can men. When Luis Alberto Urrea returns to his former home in Tijuana he reunites with his younger friend, who is still a resident of the city's garbage dump, and shows her how to dream. And in the process, demonstrates what it means to be a compadre in this day and age.

Although writers are often known to be solitary and private people, without a comadre willing to back them through crucial years of self-discovery, making their way in the U.S. might have been utterly impossible. In these twelve candid and thought-provoking stories chock-full of devourable morsels of wisdom, perhaps you too will recognize your own comadre in your life. If this is so, then you are one lucky person, and if you're in need of finding that special friend, now you know where to find her, comadre. You can count on us.

Nora de Hoyos Comstock, PhD
President & CEO
Las Comadres Para Las Americas
www.lascomadres.org

LAS COMAIS

Esmeralda Santiago

In my first memory of my mother's comadres, they're waiting for us at the school gate. Mami, doña Zena, and doña Ana wore home-sewn cotton dresses, the thin fabric pressing against their pregnant bellies, the hems flapping against their skinny legs. Around them, toddlers chased each other and raised dust clouds in their wakes. Near them stood doña Lola, tall and long-limbed, her deliberate movements a choreographed dance.

As soon as the teacher rang the bell, we ran toward our mothers, jabbering about our day, challenging one another's versions. The moment we turned the corner of the schoolyard, we helped the comadres to take their shoes off, and did the same to ours. Shoes were a luxury, and to make them last, we all walked barefoot, and wore shoes only when "*gente*" could see us. *Gente* were people who didn't live in the barrio: our teachers in the two-room schoolhouse, for instance. My younger siblings and friends skipped and ran down the dirt road toward home, but las comadres ambled behind, every once in a while calling one of us to stop doing this or that, and if we didn't, swatting our heads with their free hands or with a shoe. This is what parents did then, when mothers and fathers had no idea that we could be psychologically (if not physically) scarred by their quick hands.

I was as playful and energetic as every other child in that barrio, but I didn't join my cohorts. I hung back, preferring to walk with the mothers so that I could listen in on their conversations.

Doña Zena was the eldest of the comadres, taller than Mami or doña Ana.

"Mira nene, deja eso, por Dios y Nuestra Señora."

Every sentence she uttered invoked God and the Virgin and she was a walking encyclopedia of saints, prophets, and holy obligations. We children knew not to make noise near her house on Saturdays because she and her family spent most of the day in prayer.

"Tres curas y una monja . . ." doña Ana started. She was shorter than Mami, broad shouldered, with an easy smile and a laughing voice. She loved riddles and jokes, but when she began her story, Mami shooed me away because doña Ana's jokes were often naughty.

Mami was younger than doña Zena and doña Ana. By the year I started elementary school at six, she was twenty-four and already had three children younger than me and another on the way. She wore her black hair in a curly ponytail to her waist, and walked with a straight back that made her seem proud.

As we reached doña Zena's gate, I slowed to smell the air. Her house was surrounded by flowering plants, and her porch was festooned with morning glory vines and potted geraniums, sweetly perfumed. Her daughters, who were a little older than I was, went inside, but doña Zena stopped to clip flowers from the hibiscus hedge.

Further down was doña Ana's, the only house on this end of the barrio built from cement, its broad porch facing the road. From her pasture, her cow mooed, and squawks and screeches came from behind the banana grove, where her husband and sons kept fighting cocks.

Ours was the last gate before the barrio curved toward the funnel end. The house was a hodgepodge of coconut palm fronds, rusty metal sheets, and cardboard. My father had built a cement foundation around the perimeter of the current structure, but after many Sundays, the cinderblock walls only reached to my knees. In the back was the kitchen shed with the three stones that formed the *fogón*, its embers blinking and smoking. Huge drums under the eaves captured water for washing and bathing. On the far edge of the rear yard was the latrine, built from palm fronds.

Delsa, Norma, and Hector chased each other into the front yard. I went inside to take off my uniform, another luxury. I was not allowed to eat or drink anything while wearing it except during lunch in the school cafeteria, and I'd better make sure not to spill on it or I'd get a swat from Mami's shoe.

As I changed, doña Lola and Mami ladled from the pot of chicken *asopao* she'd brought earlier. My sisters and brother sat on the nearby felled tree trunk near the kitchen shed. Mami told me to watch the others and then went inside the house with doña Lola. From the tree trunk, I could see doña Lola gently pressing around Mami's belly.

"It won't be long, *mi'ja*," she told her. "The baby has already turned."

Of the three neighbors, doña Lola was my favorite. She lived down the road, in a wooden house with a corrugated zinc roof. She tended gardens for cooking and medicinal plants, fruit trees, and a shady grove where she grew coffee. I often helped her harvest the plump, red berries, which she dried under the sun on her metal roof. She roasted them in small batches in a huge cast-iron skillet. Whenever Mami came over, doña Lola handed me the coffee grinder as she settled the pot full of rainwater over the orange embers of the *fogón*. I sat on a stump with the grinder between my knees, turning the handle slowly until the little drawer underneath was full of the fragrant black grounds. Doña Lola's kitchen, like ours, was a separate shack, and garlands of dried herbs and twigs dangled from the beams. She was the barrio midwife and healer, consulted for ailments from machete wounds to stomachaches to lovesickness.

We were taught to add the honorific *doña* to women's first names, but Mami called them *comais*—comadres. The way she addressed them, so different from ours, indicated there was a special relationship between the women that we children didn't share.

Comai Lola was the eldest of the comadres, all of whom lived shouting distance from each other. Comai Zena and comai Ana were in their twenties, but comai Lola had adult sons and daughters scattered along the path from the main road to the furthest corner of Barrio Macún. Comai Lola was sinewy and wore her gray hair braided then wrapped around her head like a crown. I admired her quiet dignity and how she seemed to be dancing when standing still.

When we visited comai Ana, Mami sat on the cement porch sewing, talking, and laughing more than any other time. Sometimes she laughed until she cried, but often the laughter became sad tears and comai Ana rubbed her shoulders and softened her voice to say things I couldn't hear.

We didn't see doña Zena as much as the other comadres, because she was always praying, and we shouldn't disturb her.

When Mami was sad, however, or after she'd had an argument with us or with Papi, she called on comai Zena, cocooned in the scent of flowers on her porch, and they prayed together.

I was jealous of the hours Mami spent with the comadrcs, how they could talk about things I was not supposed to know or hear. But I was a curious . . . actually, a nosy child. My sisters and brother played nearby but I sidled close enough to the comadres when Mami was with them, or when they came over, or at the public fountain where we filled buckets for drinking water.

That's where I first heard that Mami grew up in San Juan. It was why she hated the *campo,* and why she was terrified of snakes. Before going to bed, she swept the floors and shook the hammocks and blankets, afraid that snakes lurked in the shadowy corners. Because she was scared of them, Mami saw a snake everywhere. They crossed her path toward the pigpen, or she surprised them coiled among the vines when she went to dig for sweet potatoes or slithering along the annatto bushes, and once, she claimed, she found a snake wrapped around the carved post of her and Papi's four-poster bed. When she saw a snake, she began to shake and scream, pointing where she saw it, but when we came to look, the snake had always disappeared into the brush. We didn't really believe that she'd seen one. None of us ever did.

After sighting a snake, Mami stood for a while, looking near her feet fearfully and rubbing her goose bumps.

Comai Lola insisted that there was nothing to be afraid of; there were no venomous snakes in Puerto Rico.

"Es que le tengo asco, " Mami said, grimacing in disgust.

Mami also worried about ghosts and spirits and was afraid of the long nights, noisy with the screeches, chirrups, and croaks of nocturnal animals. Electricity had not arrived in the barrio, so once the sun set, we lived within the quivering circles shaped by gas lamps. Bats and huge flying insects buzzed over our heads even inside the house, and brown toads jumped from the dark corners after she'd closed the doors and windows.

"Don't be afraid of the toads, *mi'ja*," comai Lola told her, "they eat the flies and mosquitoes."

"The smallest, peskiest insect is a gift from God," comai Zena assured her.

"That reminds me of the story of the prince who was a frog," comai Ana started, and Mami sent me on a pointless errand even though I'd heard that story, and it wasn't naughty.

When Mami's labor pains began, she sent me to alert her comadres. We were herded to doña Zena's, to be watched by her daughters. From the fragrant porch I could hear Mami's screams. When it was dark, I sneaked off and peeped through the space between two boards of our house. The flames from two oil lamps bathed the single room in golden light that formed fabulous shadows against the uneven walls. Comai Lola and comai Zena supported Mami so she could walk around the room. Strands of her hair were matted against her forehead, cheeks, neck, and shoulders. She was my mother, but her grimaces had changed her face into a bizarre mask.

"*Ayúdame Dios santo,*" Mami cried, and doubled over, holding her belly.

The women helped her stand, rubbed her back and shoulders, and muttered encouraging words. Comai Ana came in from the kitchen carrying a panful of hot water that she poured into a large enameled bowl I'd seen in comai Lola's kitchen. They guided Mami toward the bed. Behind me I heard comai Zena's eldest daughter calling my name, and I ran.

Mami often complained that she was trapped in a jungle, struggling alone with her children in a shack with no lights, no running water, no money or any way to earn it. Everything that was wrong with her life, she said to the *comais,* was due to my father. Papi, like the other men in Macún, worked in towns far from the barrio or in the endless sugarcane fields. The fathers were like apparitions. They were around on Sundays and on holidays, but the rest of the time, left home before the sun rose and returned after the children went to bed. There were a few old men and women in Macún, but the barrio was mostly populated by mothers with young children, and I'd overheard that every one of their husbands was as feckless as Papi.

Although the comadres often complained to each other about their men, they treated the compadres like princes. On Saturday after work, the *compais* got together at the *colmado* on the main road, to drink beer, play dominoes, listen to the jukebox. They wore white starched shirts, and pants with sharp creases down the front that their wives had pressed with heavy black irons. When they were home, their meals were served before anyone else's and their wives and children tiptoed near them until they were noticed. The fathers, who were never there, were more powerful than our mothers, who never went anywhere. "Wait until your father comes home," kept us in line, aware that his leather belt raised red welts on legs and buttocks for infractions our mothers had already punished with hands or a switch.

Decades later, I have strong memories of the comadres, but can't conjure a single one of their husbands. They were mysterious, and we children were afraid of them. Their absence made the bond between the *comais* stronger. The women were co-mothers to the passel of children who came in and out of each other's yards and homes to play, to relay messages, to ask to borrow a bit of sugar, to stay out of the rain, to have a cut or scrape treated. We children knew that there were many eyes on us, each comadre looking out for her children and those of her *comais*.

That's not to say that this community of women and children was idyllic or in any way utopian. The comadres were strong-willed women who'd come together by circumstance, not choice. They were considerate and obliging, but also bickered and gossiped, criticized one another, sometimes taking the opposing side from what I expected.

After she'd had seven children, and the youngest, Raymond, was four, Mami found a job in a garment factory in the next town. The comadres didn't approve of her working outside her home. They ridiculed her for wearing a girdle, straight skirts, and high heels. They made nasty comments about how she curled her hair, powdered and colored her cheeks, and wore lipstick. They claimed she abandoned her children, and complained that we were running wild around the barrio. It was true that with Mami at work we were freer of her strict rules, but we weren't alone. Mami hired doña Ana's daughter to watch and feed us until she came home from work.

They could be spiteful, but the comadres couldn't hold grudges for long because they might need each other at any moment. When comai Zena's father fell ill, the comadres took turns nursing him, washing the linens, offering meals from their kitchens. It was the comadres who prepared the body and the house for the wake, and led the novenas after the funeral.

One year, the comadres and their families, including the husbands, hunkered behind the reinforced doors and windows of comai Ana's cement house. The hurricane that raced through Puerto Rico that summer devastated the vegetable plots and gardens, destroyed homes, killed cattle, pigs, and horses, and felled fruit trees in every direction. Over the next weeks, the comadres shared what was in their pantries. Their husbands and sons formed work brigades to rebuild one another's houses. The comadres organized the children to pick branches for kindling, and to clear the detritus the hurricane had deposited in our yards and on the road.

Near the mango tree, I found a strange metal object with four wheels. Papi said it was a roller skate and guessed this one had flown in the hurricane's winds all the way from San Juan, where there were sidewalks. He gave me a cord so that I could tie it to my foot. Because there was no pavement until we reached the main road, the only place where I could ride my roller skate was on doña Ana's cement porch. Mami held me as I balanced on one leg, and soon I was able to ride back and forth without falling. When tired of riding on the right leg, I switched to the left foot. The other kids lined up to take rides on the skate, and we spent hours rolling from here to there and back on doña Ana's porch. We tried to outdo one another with tricks. We squatted over the skate with the free leg in front, or in our version of a ballet arabesque, balancing while the other leg stretched behind. The comadres watched and applauded, but just as often, had to pick us up from the hard floor when a particular *maroma* didn't quite work as we had hoped.

"*Sana, sana, colita de rana, si no sana hoy, se sanará mañana.*"

Somehow a comadre's voice singing a silly rhyme made us feel better, especially when accompanied by a tight hug and a kiss.

Fifteen years after we left Puerto Rico I went back to Barrio Macún. Doña Zena still lived in the same house surrounded by flowers, her porch decorated with colorful geraniums and morning glories. Her wooly hair was streaked with white, and her hands were scarred and work worn, with prominent knuckles. She blessed me, thanking saints and virgins whose efforts, she said, had helped me to survive the rigors of New York, and would continue to guide and protect me when I return. I was surprised at the raspy sound of her voice, and a bit annoyed by her chiding me for being still single and childless at twenty-eight.

Doña Ana didn't have the house with the cement porch where I'd honed my skills as a one-skate skater. A highway now crossed her pasture, and her house, doña Lola's, and ours had been demolished. Doña Ana now lived right next to the school and sold candy, drinks, school supplies, and trinkets wrapped in cellophane from a shack in the yard. As I sipped on a cold soda, she told me a couple of ribald jokes that I could now understand, and laughed with her, feeling as if I had joined a club that had been closed to me as a child.

I was curious to see doña Lola. The longer I lived in the United States, the more I missed her. To me she represented the Puerto Rican *jíbara*, the self-sufficient countrywoman, knowledgeable about, and in harmony with, her surroundings; and as a healer and midwife, in touch with every aspect of the birth, life, and death of every person in Barrio Macún. She now lived at the end of a narrow path lined by medicinal plants and fruit trees. She showed me the cement corral where she kept land crabs. Further down was her pigsty, and a little further, her goat was tied to a stake. Her kitchen was a separate shack that looked pretty much the same as the one I remembered, with a three-stone *fogón* in the corner, the embers smoldering, and dried herbs tied to the beams.

"Here you go," she handed me the same coffee grinder I'd used as a child. I found the stump just outside the kitchen and turned the handle, breathing in the fragrance of the smoky home-roasted beans, as doña Lola told me that her sons and daughters had emigrated to New York and Chicago. They wrote often, but a neighbor had to read the letters because she didn't know how to read or write. Most of the residents of the barrio were newcomers and she didn't know many of them.

"I wish things in Puerto Rico were the same as when I was a child," I sighed, "when we were one huge family."

"Ay, no, *mi'ja*, don't waste precious time wishing for the past. If you do, you'll wake some morning to realize that you've spent your life wishing."

She made the coffee the old-fashioned way in an enameled pot, dropping the grounds into the boiling water, then filtering them through a darkly stained flannel sock with a patinated wooden handle. We sat on her porch, sipping the delicious brew. Against the far wall of the room behind me there were stacks of unopened boxes of appliances.

"What are those, doña Lola?"

"Oh, gifts from my children and grandchildren."

"Why do you keep them in the boxes?"

"I don't know what most of those contraptions do. I don't have electricity."

"Why not sell them, or give them away?"

"They remind me of them," she said.

The comadres helped Mami at a place and time when she most needed them. Now over eighty, crusty and independent, she argues that comai Ana, comai Zena, and comai Lola didn't do as much as I think they did. Perhaps Mami undermines their influence with the same jealousy I felt when she spent too much time with them.

It's difficult to imagine what our lives might have been if the three comadres had not befriended Mami when she needed to cope with a situation that challenged her beyond her expectations and knowledge. Comai Ana's jokes and stories made Mami laugh when she'd be more likely to cry. Comai Zena's prayers were soothing when she was most confused or despairing. And comai Lola became a surrogate mother who taught her about the *campo*, delivered her babies, and showed that it was possible to live in oneness with her environment.

It didn't surprise me that when things didn't work out as she'd hoped in New York, Mami returned to Barrio Macún

seven years after we'd left. With the other comadres, she nursed
doña Ana's daughter during her last painful months before she
died of cancer. A few years later, Mami married the widower
and raised his young children with the same fierce protective-
ness as her own.

When I was a young mother, I often remembered the three comadres and wished that I could call upon their humor, faith, and
knowledge. My husband and I had settled in a suburban village
south of Boston where I often felt that I was the only foreign
person. Then I met the Latinas who congregated in the playground sharing stories. As an American citizen, as an educated
professional, as the mother of the children climbing the mon-
key bars, I did not share the same legal, job, social, or economic
circumstances as the nannies. But we all were lonely, alienated
from where we lived, and often felt uneasy under the curious,
and sometimes hostile, glances of our neighbors who frequently
asked us where we were from.

"I always tell them I come from Chelsea," Leonor said, nam-
ing the town north of Boston where she lived from Friday af-
ternoons to Monday mornings, when she was off from nanny
duty. We could laugh at the truthful answer, and her refusal to
accept that she didn't belong where she now was, instead of El
Salvador, where she was born.

Regardless of our differences, we listened and learned from
each other, supported and encouraged each others' efforts as we
managed new lives in the United States. We'd all grown up in
Latin America and had more in common with each other than

with our *norteamericano* neighbors. We understood the concept of comadrazgo—the principle that all mothers of a community share responsibility for raising everyone's children—instilled by our mothers' relationships with their comadres. I didn't call them *comais,* but they provided the same solace that Mami received from comai Ana, comai Zena, and comai Lola when she felt a stranger in a new land.

Mami's three comadres in Barrio Macún have passed away, but their lessons of camaraderie, generosity, faith, and wry humor continue to inspire me. Having had them in my life, I knew how crucial it was for women to join in solidarity, to work toward common goals, to find comfort in each other. My life has been informed and enriched by the example set by comai Ana, comai Zena, and comai Lola.

I will never forget the three comadres standing on the periphery of the sunny schoolyard, their pregnant bellies carrying the future. They have had an impact beyond their lives. When they were Mami's friends, the *comais* had no idea that they were models to her child, and none of us ever imagined that they would become characters in memoirs and novels that same intrepid girl would someday write. They have become the prototypes for womanhood, and their lives and lessons reverberate through my work and through my life.

EVERY DAY
OF HER LIFE

Carolina De Robertis

I.

I taught Leila the word comadre a year and a half before she died. She loved it instantly. The term encapsulated what she already knew about women, about friendship, community, the curve and flavor of an exuberant, largehearted life. The moment she learned the word, it was already home.

We had been friends then for three years, ever since we met at our MFA in creative writing. But it seemed as though we'd known each other for much longer—for decades, or perhaps lifetimes. We'd shared such intimate corners of our souls. We'd dared and stretched and read and dreamed together, pushed our written words as far as we could take them and then further; we opened our deepest sources of vulnerability and courage. We drew sustenance from each other when our novels-in-progress overwhelmed us or felt like an irreparable mess, reminding each other of why we wrote; our desire to voice stories that might otherwise go untold.

Leila used the word comadre with me, but she also shared it with women friends of other backgrounds, presenting it as a rich treasure offered up by Latino culture, a gift for those who resonate with it throughout global tribes. She embraced the term with such peerless passion that, whenever I hear it, I see her face.

2.

Since her death, Leila's presence in my life has continued to grow. My house, which I bought two months before she died, is suffused with reminders of her. The olive tree in the yard whose fruits she said I had to learn to cure (*I'll teach you*, she said, both of us assuming a second half to that sentence, *one day when I'm better*); bread from the local bakery she first told me about; the single Mediterranean tile she gave me as a housewarming gift that sits on the kitchen counter and murmurs to me of grief and of faraway homelands, both hers and mine. Sometimes, when I read intriguing articles online, my fingers still itch to forward them to her, disbelieving that she's left for a place whose connectivity is beyond my computer's ability to decipher. Often, in the midst of an adventure—an inspiring book fair, a party full of laughter, a graciously presented meal steeped in ancestral traditions—I find myself thinking, *Oh Leila, you would love this,* as though forming those words in my mind could make her appear beside me. And, sometimes, I feel that she does appear, and her radiance is beautiful. I could wrap it around me in a great, bright shawl. But it is still not Leila standing physically in a room, filling it completely as she used to do, standing an elegant six feet tall, with her big voice and gregarious ways that could instantly warm everyone around her. Feeling her spirit's presence is not the same as having her here, alive, embodied. It will never be the same.

And there it is, the terrible, obvious truth about life: All of it passes, each moment, each joy, even the body itself—and nothing will ever be the same.

3.

Co-*madre*.

Co-mother.

The comadre steps in when her beloved friend can no longer care for her child. She takes the child into her home, opens her arms, adopts her dear friend's progeny and raises it as though it were her own.

Leila left two young sons when she died, but they did not need taking in. Their father's love is as solid as bedrock. It is her other child, the novel she was working on, that cried out to be held and nurtured, to be brought into another home.

And so, for these two years since Leila's death, along with her widower and one other friend, I have been coediting the gorgeous unfinished book she left behind, a sprawling portrait of her native Lebanon. Every time I enter those pages, I see new things about Leila, what she loved and feared and longed for, her most secret and treasured visions. I am becoming more intimate with her. Our friendship is still in the present tense. She is not only inside my heart, but also inside my days, my creative process, those unlit layers of the soul that are engaged by writing, stories, dreams. She is still teaching me about what it means to write, what it means to live, who she really was and who I can continue to become.

4.

Sometimes, it's exhilarating to work on Leila's book. At other times, it's painful. Novels require a tremendous amount of heavy lifting to become completely polished, and Leila isn't here to flesh out scenes, add context, or explain loopholes in the plot—all those tasks that fall to the novelist in the last year or three of working on a novel. In the best moments, I've felt transported, because if reading is a way of communing with an author's consciousness, then editing an author's work can be even more intimate, a couple's dance for the spirit. When I am inside Leila's book, sensing what is missing and what needs to come next, I feel her with me, inside my mind, humming, and all I have to do is record what I hear in her tune. In the worst moments, I have stared at glaring holes in the manuscript and felt helpless to fill them myself, because I am not Leila, I don't have her voice. *You should be here to do this,* I rage, *not me*—and then I feel guilty for the thought.

Guilty because, first of all, I chose to take part in editing her book posthumously. It's an honor to be part of this. I could walk out on the arrangement anytime. So how dare I complain about a task I am choosing? (Because if you hadn't died, Leila, I wouldn't have had to choose it. I want to unchoose it and have you here instead.)

Secondly, it's unfair to direct the rage at her. I should be hurling it toward death itself. Leila didn't want to die. That's an understatement: Leila's desire for life was a tsunami that made death look like a clutch of pebbles, easily drowned. She fought unbelievably hard. I saw her do it. In her last month, she was measuring her pee and her water intake to the milliliter so that she could drink as much as possible to slake her thirst without overloading her failing liver and kidneys. She made her own chart, in the hospital, on the back of a piece of scratch paper she asked a nurse to give to her. She showed it to me the day I came to visit her in the hospital, when her legs were swollen thick and firm and yellow from jaundice; the skin stretched so taut by the swelling, I feared it might burst and explode her raw self into the room. On that day, she held court in her hospital bed, in that unerringly-gracious-hostess way of hers, telling stories about permaculture and creative epiphanies and literature, inquiring about my baby and my book tour, and mentioning, almost as an aside, that her oncologist had told her she'd be released from the hospital, not because she was better, but because there was nothing more they could do.

"She seemed so worked up," Leila said, almost bemused. "But I have no plans to die. I'm organizing a Reiki healing circle at my mother's church. Twenty Reiki masters offering me healing all at once. How about that? So I don't see this as the end. I'm not going anywhere."

She sounded so sure. She looked so ill. And yet, if she had told me, in that tone, that purple dragons were going to fly down from the moon that very evening, I would have joyously believed her.

Leila died three weeks later.

5.

During that same hospital stay, Leila had been stranded on the first floor after a series of tests. She was wheeled there on a gurney because she couldn't walk anymore, or so she'd been told. Once the tests were done, the technician left her in the hallway to be picked up. Only nobody came. The technicians had gone on their lunch break and forgotten her. She lay there for over an hour, waiting, and nobody came by whom she could ask for help. She called out; nothing.

Leila finally dragged herself off the gurney and walked down the hall, dragging Spike, as she'd named the wheeled stand that held her intravenous fluids. It took her ten minutes and a lot of pain. She reached the elevator and rose to her floor.

As she and Spike approached the nurses' station, Leila shouted, in her characteristically forceful voice:

"HERE—COMES—TROUBLE!"

6.

When editing a book, ruthless decisions must be made. It is the only way through the woods of chaos into the great plains of coherence. How can we make those decisions on Leila's behalf? How can we define her work and at the same time keep it true to her vision? How can we possibly tap that unshakable secret force that impelled Leila to devote the last four years of her life to creating this book?

Novels come from a place of profound inner urgency; they have to do so in order to come alive. At least, that's the only way I know to go about it. The two novels I've written so far were both fueled by the hunger to reconnect with my nation of origin, to explore questions about violence and passion and courage and survival, and to carve a space in the world for those who are perceived not to belong. Which was, in part, a way of carving space for myself, of forging a home in this world. I wrote from my ancestral stories while my parents were cutting me out of their lives for marrying a woman, back when such a marriage had nothing legal to it—civil disobedience in white silk. I wrote while working full-time as a rape crisis counselor, founding a program for Latinas who'd survived sexual assault, and then both working and paying my way through graduate school. I thought I knew a thing or two about adversity and persistence.

But I have never written a novel while slowly losing a battle with cancer. So what do I know about urgency?

7.

Leila's book is called *Noah's Crow*. It tells the story of Donia, a Lebanese-American woman who returns to her father's native village in 1995 to learn what happened to the body of her grandmother, who disappeared during Lebanon's long civil war. Her journey is interwoven with stories of the past—her grandmother's brutal removal from school and ensuing life as a young bride; her father's trajectory from farmer's son to academic prodigy to emigrant engineer with a dream of rebuilding his beloved homeland; her Christian cousin's forbidden love with a Palestinian Muslim, who, like her, supports a movement for unity among peoples; the wrenching losses and brave acts of survival of the war that raged from 1975 to 1990. It is a lush novel, sensuous with the scents and sounds and flavors of Lebanon, rich with grief and hope and passion for a village rooted in ancient heritage, torn by violence, and resilient as the verdant weeds that grow in bombed-out buildings.

It reads like a love letter to Lebanon.

My first novel was a love letter, too, only to Uruguay, a very different nation in a very different part of the world, but also a homeland that, like Leila's Lebanon, felt both intimate and far. We were both daughters of immigrants, and we both turned to the novel as a container for mapping our inheritance, so we could see it, hold it, grapple with it, trace its contours on the page.

In this way, Leila and I were sisters.

8.

We were sisters from the beginning. As soon as we met, in our first semester at Mills College, we had the sort of connection that caused us to lose track of time when we talked. I was thirty years old; she was forty-three. I saw her as a stable, mature woman, established in her life. She owned her own home, a remarkable feat in the Bay Area that I had, at the time, given up as impossible to ever achieve. She had two small boys, while I did not yet have children (though I longed for them). She kept a highly popular blog entitled "Dove's Eye View: An Arab-American Woman Sees Signs of Hope," where she posted conscious and compassionate reflections on Middle Eastern affairs, as well as sumptuous recipes that she wove in with the following motto: "When there's no hope left, you can always make dinner." Her online political writing was deeply important to her, but the desire to write fiction had always been there too, under the surface. Then, a cancer diagnosis had focused her intentions. In the thick of treatments, she stared death in the face and thought hard about what unfinished business she had on earth. She re-arranged her life to pursue an MFA and write the novel she'd been carrying inside her for years. By the time she started the program, the cancer was in remission; she was healthy, vibrant, and ready to chase down her dream.

Cancer got me here to write my novel, she would sometimes say.

9.

Leila and I, along with a few other friends at our MFA program, found ourselves swept up in a series of courses that transformed and expanded our writing in ways we had not imagined possible. The teacher, Micheline Aharonian Marcom, an incandescent writer of Armenian origin, brought an innovative method to the classroom. We read books from a dizzying range of styles, cultures, and historical eras, and discussed them through the lens of what they did for us—or to us—as writers, striving to engage faculties beyond the intellect, approaching the conversation as a magic carpet ride into the mysterious art of writing. Then we took turns standing up and reading fresh work directly inspired by the book we'd read. We entered a kind of communion with the texts and with each other's words, through which our own work grew and flourished. These courses bucked the way creative writing courses are usually taught in contemporary U.S. universities, favoring an approach at once intuitive and communal, unique and yet true to what writers and storytellers have done since the beginning of time.

It was just what Leila and I had both been looking for. We

kept returning to Micheline's classes, semester after semester, devouring Aeschylus and Faulkner, Calvino and Duras, Borges and Calasso, Kawabata and Anne Carson, Kafka and Jung, García Márquez and Kadare and many others, letting them infuse our writing and weave us into a circle of writers on fire.

Students took turns being "hosts" for the evening. Hosts were charged with sparking discussion, setting the tone, and bringing food and wine to share with their fellow students. Because the method was so experiential, the enthusiasm of the host had a tremendous impact on the class.

Leila was among the first to host. She put us all to shame. We were reading the *Thousand and One Nights*. She spread out an intricately patterned tablecloth she had brought over from Lebanon. She set out beautiful ceramic dishes and filled them with a variety of olives, lemon chicken, dolmas, hummus, baba ghanoush, za'atar, pita bread, and olive oil. She lit candles and turned off the lights. As we started eating, she explained the meaning of each food, the story behind each delicacy and serving dish. She must have spent all day preparing, and we all felt the generosity of her gifts and the subtle power of her invocation. Her facilitation of our discussion was just as exuberant. That night's conversation was unforgettable to anyone who had the good fortune to attend. We not only talked about the *Thousand and One Nights*, we *entered* them; Shahrazad's voice hummed under the surface of our conversation, that voice with which she'd told stories to save her own life and the lives of all the women of her land. Give everything to your stories, I felt her saying. Hurl all the force you've been given into what you have to say. The power of storytelling is as ancient as the trees these olives came from, as the fires that baked this bread. And it feeds you just as much as they do. Eat, drink, listen. These tales are older than you know.

Leila had set the bar high for the rest of us. If it hadn't been for her, our classes might have devolved into the measly bags-of-chips offerings that so often occur among busy contemporary graduate students. But after the *Thousand and One Nights*, the writers in our classes cooked, dreamed, innovated, laid artful tables, and shared foods from their cultural heritages or from the heritages of the authors we were reading. Throughout graduate school, Leila's enthusiasm and commitment set the tone, abundant and utterly infectious.

10.

Halfway through our MFA program, in the summer of 2006, Leila's father died of cancer, and war broke out between Israel and Lebanon. Those two events, twisted together, formed a terrible rope of grief for Leila. It became difficult for her to concentrate on her novel. She found herself online often, reading wrenching reports, commenting fiercely on blogs around the world, and writing posts of her own. On her blog, she wrote commentaries that drew readership from across the globe, and that amplified the truths behind the headlines, and made eloquent appeals for peace.

And yet, the war and her father's death had made the long, slow work of the novel more urgent than ever. Great human events can't be fully captured in news headlines, important as they are. Novels have a particular power to convey the full intimate resonance of an experience such as war. I believe that Leila sensed this, too. Her book had been born out of her original grief over the Lebanese Civil War, which destroyed her father's beloved village and took the life of her own grandmother, whose remains were never found. Her blog posts were potent and important, but it would take fiction to give full voice to what she had to say.

In her second and final MFA year, Leila rallied and plunged back into her book.

II.

After graduation, Leila, six other writers, and I continued to meet on our own. The majority of us happened to be daughters of immigrants, which gave us a powerful container in which to craft books that evoked our nations of origin—Japan, Guatemala, the Philippines, Lebanon, Uruguay. We came together in each other's homes, took turns cooking dinner, read books and discussed them, dreamed, connected, read work aloud, and exchanged inspiration and support.

Leila was a beacon in our group, an organizing force. She would write us big, inspired emails, often out of the blue, ruminating on creativity or literature or philosophy or the links between art and social change, and they always began the exact same way:

"Darlings—"

With that single word she swept us up in the great embrace of her luminous mind, and transformed us from an ordinary cluster of writers into our very own twenty-first-century, California-style, international version of the Bloomsbury Group.

A year into that period, her cancer returned.

12.

At that same time, I became pregnant and the rights to my first novel sold, the realization of two lifelong dreams. Leila was thrilled for me. It is possible for envy to embitter friendships between writers—or simply between women—but Leila gave me only love and joy.

As a mother, she showered me with encouragement and tips from her own life.

As a fellow writer, she took me out to lunch to celebrate the book deal. Later that day, she announced it on her blog, saying she was "over the moon," and cheering me on in beautiful terms, perhaps the most beautiful being the warmth with which she referred to me, for all to see, as her comadre.

There have been times since Leila's death when I have searched my own name online just to ensure that her post still appears, as though that presence kept one more link between us on this earth.

13.

I attended the Reiki healing circle at Leila's mother's church. It was the last time I ever saw her. She was extremely bloated from her liver's inability to remove fluids from her system. Her skin was dark yellow from jaundice. Children, she told me that day, had run away from her in fear. And yet she sat, gracious hostess, in her wheelchair beside her husband David, radiating a kind and welcoming smile that must have taken God knows how much energy to sustain. Because she was Leila Abu-Saba every day of her life.

The chapel was packed. The minister invited everyone who had received Reiki attunement to come forward and put their hands on Leila as the remainder of the congregants sang. I went up to the front, and was just able to reach the tips of my fingers to her back through the crowd of well-wishing healers. A gentle chant filled the room. Several attendees were weeping, though trying hard to fight it. They had not been prepared to see Leila so sick.

At the close of the chant, Leila turned to us behind her and said, "Thank you, thank you, thank you," the way you might thank a sweet old aunt for a hand-knit sweater you know won't fit.

That same night, she changed her Facebook profile picture to a photo of her father. He had been dead now for three years, and she missed him with all her soul.

If she didn't know before, she certainly knew then: Wherever her father was, she was headed there soon, and the journey could not be stopped.

14.

When Leila was in hospice care, and clearly in her final days, Micheline, who since graduation had become a friend, wrote me an email. She, too, was heartbroken over Leila's decline. She was going to offer to edit Leila's book posthumously, and help get it published. Would I do it with her? I said yes. The whole of my being rushed into that yes. Another friend, Sara Campos, took the message to Leila's bedside. Leila accepted the offer with the faculties she had left; she nodded emphatically and said a few excited words, riding a burst of energy.

Once that promise had been made—once Leila knew her manuscript would have someone to care for it just as her husband would care for the boys—she finally let go of the struggle. That day, she lost the ability to speak. Three days later, she passed peacefully with friends at her side.

15.

David asked me to speak at Leila's memorial service specifically on her life as a novelist, a part of her that was intrinsic to who she was and yet not known to all who loved her.

When I arrived at the service—another packed chapel—I discovered there were only three people on the program. Her husband. Her brother. And me. I was shocked by this; there were so many people who had known Leila longer. She had other relatives, and many devoted friends. I felt humbled, tongue-tied. How could I speak? But I had to do it—not for myself, but for her writing. I had brought a poem that she wrote in the hospital, and an excerpt from her novel, in which the narrator ruminates on the beauty of the world, even in the face of death. Leila's written words were an enormous part of who she was, and what she left us. They had to be shared.

Somehow, I managed to get through all but the last thirty seconds without tears.

16.

Micheline spearheaded another, more literary memorial on the Mills campus for faculty, fellow students, and Leila's family. We—Leila's writer friends—brought candles and flowers and elegant food, as she would have liked for us to do. We took turns going to the podium and reading in Leila's name: Some of us read from her writings, others from our own work, still others from published texts that resonated with the moment. We read in candlelight. We read through tears. We laughed as a former professor, who'd returned to campus especially for this service, read a story of Leila's that crackled with humor. All the while, an enormous photograph of Leila sat on a chair, wreathed in flowers, beaming and flickering in the light of many small flames.

There was such grief in the room.

Grief is what love becomes when people die. I had always imagined the two to be utterly different emotions, grief and love, but I was wrong. One transmutes into the other. They are different faces of the same essential force, so that the more you love before death, the more you will grieve after.

Yet another thing I've learned from Leila: Strip Grief of her clothes and see her naked—her name is Love.

17.

When Micheline, David, and I embarked on our work on Leila's novel, we had no road map, no clear plan. None of us had done such a thing before. We were in utterly new territory.

The manuscript came to us riddled with repetition, contradictions, and rough exploratory writing that Leila clearly still intended to return to and expand. The sections were saved out of order, in an idiosyncratic maze that could only have made sense to her. In other words, the manuscript was a mess.

We started with the big picture. First, we placed the parts in an order that generally reflected what we knew of her intention for the structure of the novel. Then we went into the chapters, one by one, and edited them, making stylistic and structural decisions (the protagonist will speak in first person; the dead will speak in italics). We hacked out long swaths of underdeveloped prose. We named chapters and minor characters. We realized that parts were not working in the structure we'd created, and rearranged them until they sang out more clearly. Finally, toward the end, we grew bold and did what the book demanded and what we finally felt the authority (*author-ity*) to do: We created dialogue where it was missing, killed characters who didn't serve the plot, and wrote in the essential ligaments—brief scenes, interior thoughts, closing and opening sentences—that could make the book cohere.

At first I thought the work on Leila's novel would be mostly editorial, a caring outside eye to polish what was already there. But over the past two years, we have crossed the line from editors to writers, cutting and writing and rewriting as relentlessly as though the book were our own. I have come to adopt *Noah's Crow* and give it the same love and devotion and stern hand that I bring to my own novels.

We worked for two years. We held many five-hour meetings, fueled by Thai takeout and copious coffee, during which we wrote and wrote and laughed and worked and came to know the intimate rhythms of each other's minds. By the end, we'd stopped rotating homes and met every time at David's house, which will always be Leila's house to me. The hours sped by. Considering the deep solitude in which novel writing usually takes place, the meetings were a rare venture into a communal approach to the labor of fiction, unlike anything I've ever experienced before or even heard of anyone else experiencing. Even in death, Leila has a gift for bringing people together.

As we worked, we listened for Leila's intentions. We let her guide us. And she did.

18.

At our very first meeting, we talked about Leila's titles for the book. She'd been leaning toward *Noah's Crow*, which I liked better than her other option, *The American Cousin*. David then said that he'd been rooting for the latter, which Leila had never told me (and thus began the many revelations).

Micheline hadn't known about either title. But she told us a story that settled the question: The day after Leila died, Micheline was too upset to write, so she went out and wandered a commercial street. She found a necklace in a store that was nothing like her usual personal style, but which called to her strongly. She bought it with Leila in her mind.

She brought the necklace from her bedroom. Bold black beads, and a single pendant with the image of a keen-eyed crow.

19.

The first line of Leila's book didn't quite fit in chapter one, but we couldn't cut it. To me, it seemed to hold what Turkish novelist Orhan Pamuk calls the "secret center" of a novel. So we placed it before that, on a page all its own:

A daughter whose village is lost to her forever belongs to the world.

Leila is in that sentence. She still breathes there. Somehow, she managed to forge a single line that sweeps up into its syllables all the sorrow and triumph and yearning of her tremendous heart.

There have been times when I've despaired about the limits of the manuscript as we received it, the holes we cannot fill, the continued writing only Leila could have done. As we approach the end of what we can do for the novel and prepare to offer it to publishers, I have to accept that we've done the best we can, done what Leila would have wanted us to do. She will never have those two extra years of health in which to finish the book on her own terms. No amount of work we do will give that time back to her.

But the heart of writing is never about the end result. What matters most is knowing, like Lily at the end of Virginia Woolf's *To the Lighthouse,* that you have done everything you could to realize your vision. And when I read that first sentence of Leila's—and other sentences in her book—and feel how much she left us, how much she gave her art, something in me silently shouts, *Leila, darling, querida, comadre, no matter what happens from this moment forward, you did it. You did it. You did.*

20.

During her final battle with cancer, Leila posted the following message on her blog:

So please, friend, bless what you have and let go of fear for the future. Today is the only day you have got. You are breathing. Enjoy your breath. You are alive. Enjoy your life. Bless everybody who comes across your path. And the work? Bless your work, too. Bless your town, your bills, your possessions. You are lucky to be here for all of it. If some of it gets taken away, fine, something else will take its place. You are an amazing confluence of billions of variables and nobody else is having your life right this minute.

And don't worry about hope. Just breathe and appreciate your breath. Everything arises from that.

I return to these lines when I seek peace over losing Leila. I remember that she loved life with a vitality that inspired others around her to do the same, that even if she didn't manage to enjoy every one of her breaths (and who the hell does?) she most certainly enjoyed many. That she cooked delicious meals and fought for peace and justice. That she birthed two beautiful boys. That she achieved that rare thing in this world, a strong and happy marriage. That she sang her love for Lebanon, and for the planet. That she wrote.

That she made the very best of her forty-seven years.

I also return to these lines when I need guidance for myself. They give me courage on the days when writing seems difficult or impossible. They remind me of what's important. They return me to my breath, to confluence. They return me home.

21.

I am inside Leila's novel. I wrap her sentences around me, supple scarves of many colors. They smell of lemons and roses, coffee and secrets, wild thyme and olive oil soap. They smell of a Lebanon I have never been to and yet, through the portal of my comadre's book, have come to love. As I move, wrapped in sentences, they rustle a mysterious language that my skin immediately understands. A language called Beauty. Her sentences speak directly to my body. They shake me awake and show me treasures. They show me what passion can forge out of the alphabet. They show me death: Leila's, and my own. Through that lens, life appears in sharp relief, with all its heat and urgency, all its roving noise, its pain and power.

Your sentences are here, Leila, and they are singing. Like you, they belong to the world.

ROAD SISTERS

Stephanie Elizondo Griest

We were hungry, we were tired, and we were lost. Daphne was in the driver's seat; I was navigating (and failing). We had been driving for three hours by that point, searching for Chilchinbito—a village so tiny, it didn't appear on our Arizona atlas. We had been told that the Cowboy family might host us for the night, but they had no phone to confirm this. And so, we were relying on faith, blind faith. Faith that the Cowboys would be home; faith they would share their homes with strangers. Otherwise, we would be sleeping on the back roads of Navajo Nation that night.

I had met Daphne a week ago, but didn't know what to make of her. Born in Brazil, raised in Venezuela and England, educated in the States, and trained in international aid relief in Africa, she was possibly the worldliest person I'd ever encountered, yet she approached each new destination on our road trip with the ecstatic enthusiasm of a novice. Her tongue was pierced and she bore a tattoo, implying a certain rebelliousness, yet she dutifully documented our mileage, filed our receipts, and cleaned out our 1981 Honda hatchback each day. She was spontaneous but methodical, free-spirited but meticulous, gregarious but intimate, equally prone to laughter and tears. Who *was* this Brazilian badass, and why was she so fascinated by my life back in Corpus Christi, Texas?

"You were a *Tigerette* in high school? Like with *pom-poms*?" she asked for the twentieth time, a smile on her lips.

Was she—to use the British phrase she'd taught me—taking the piss out of me? Or was she genuinely interested? I wasn't accustomed to someone so sophisticated being so curious.

"Yes, pom-poms. Sequined cowboy hats, too. But like I said, we weren't *cheerleaders*. We were *dancers*."

She pounded the steering wheel, shrieking in laughter.

"So," I said, trying to keep worry from seeping out my throat, "what if we don't find the Cowboys?"

"Shit, dude, we'll figure something out."

The sky was bleeding gold across the horizon. Any minute now, the sun was going to slip behind that faraway butte, and then we'd be driving in darkness. What if we missed the turn? Earlier that day, we had passed truckloads of Navajos who had stopped and poked their heads out their windows to check on us. (Bertha—our Honda—was visibly struggling along the dirt roads.) They confirmed we were headed in the right direction. Chilchinbito, straight ahead. Yet we hadn't passed more than the occasional goat in miles. And the temperature was dropping at an alarming rate. This desert valley would soon be blue cold.

But if Daphne was concerned, she didn't show it. "Let's put on some tunes. David Gray?"

I shuffled through her CD collection, neatly alphabetized between transparent sheets.

"Aha!" she said. "I see a hogan."

Off in the distance, I could make out a yurt-shaped construction of logs and clay. As we drew closer, half a dozen mobile homes appeared as well, assembled around a basketball hoop that was missing both a backboard and a net. As Daphne pulled into the settlement, Bertha sputtered to a halt and started smoking. Chilchinbito or not, we were staying here for the night.

A middle-aged Navajo woman stepped out of a doorway, curious about the commotion. She wore a T-shirt of a howling coyote and baggy jeans. No time to strategize: We hustled over to greet her. When her gaze caught mine, my mouth parched—but not Daphne's. Beaming broadly, she launched into our story. How we were from The Odyssey, a team of eight correspondents driving four cars thousands of miles across the nation to document the history so often omitted from classroom textbooks: slave rebellions, migrant workers, Japanese internment camps, the American Indian Movement. How we uploaded these stories onto a nonprofit website monitored by hundreds of thousands of K–12 students around the world. How we did all of this on a fifteen-dollar daily budget, which is why we needed to find the Cowboys of Chilchinbito, so we'd have a place to stay the night.

"The Cowboys?" the woman asked. "They're our cousins."

Daphne flung open her arms, as if to say *¡Familia!* "Danny told us we'd find you!"

Not exactly.

Over lunch at the Grand Canyon earlier that day, it had occurred to us that we had no place to stay that night. Pulling out our atlas, Daphne noticed we would be driving through the Navajo reservation, and asked our waiter if any Navajo were on staff. When he pointed out a busboy, she bum-rushed him. Five minutes later, she had all the passwords we needed: Chilchinbito, Cowboy, and Danny.

"So you need a place to stay?" the woman asked, eyebrows crinkling.

"Yes," we said in unison.

"Then stay here," she murmured, opening her door.

Daphne turned to me with a wink and a smile. When our boss broke the news of our fifteen-dollar daily stipend at orientation last week, every single one of my teammates thought it impossible—except Daphne. She thought it a challenge. And she liked challenges. Just the night before, in Vegas, she had talked the manager of a youth hostel into letting us sleep in the supply closet for half the regular rate. Girlfriend was on a roll.

We followed the woman inside her mobile home, where an ancient woman sat in a corner behind a giant loom, wearing a necklace with turquoise stones larger than my fist. Pausing in her project—a saddlebag patterned in black and white diamonds—she squinted at us with oystery eyes. From a back room appeared a man holding a wooden flute. His mouth opened in surprise at the sight of us. We all blinked at one another for an extended awkward moment. Then Daphne spun her magic.

"Oh my God! This bag is *beau*-tiful! And that flute! Did you make it? Can we hear it?"

Suddenly we were sitting together in a circle upon their linoleum floor. They treated us to a woodwind concert and a hoop dance; Daphne showed them how to samba. They shared legends that predated that entire desert valley; we regaled them with last night's adventures in Vegas. They gave us dream catchers; we outfitted them in Odyssey T-shirts. Daphne and I didn't roll out our sleeping bags until midnight. When the family turned out the lights, she reached out to stroke my arm. "I am *so* glad we are traveling together. You are *such* a cool friend," she whispered.

After a few seconds passed with no response, she hissed, "You beat me to sleep! All right, g'night."

But I wasn't sleeping. I had tucked my head inside my bag so she couldn't hear me weeping.

I discovered The Odyssey three days after the love of my life— a Che Guevara look-alike from Colombia—reached inside my chest, yanked out my heart, and incinerated it. I'm not being dramatic. The man nearly *ruined* me—twice! The first time, when we were still in college, he tried to persuade me not to study abroad in Moscow, though I'd been planning to do so for four years. *Stay here, and I'll slip a ruby ring on your finger.* And I would have, too, if he hadn't dumped me first. The second time, two years later, he lured me away from traveling around Asia after my postgrad fellowship ended in Beijing. *Come here, and we'll open a café. I want your hands all over the sweets.* So I did. Canceled a ticket to Delhi and bought one to Bogotá. Stayed a month, during which we fought incessantly. Turned out, he was an alcoholic. And a compulsive liar. And, worst of all, *machista*. I returned to Texas in despair. Had I really left Asia—for him? Now what?

Still reeling, I got online to explore a search engine I'd just learned about called Google. People said it could find *anything,* so I typed in a string of hopeful words: Travel. Adventure. World Culture. Social Justice. Change. Then I clicked "I Feel Lucky" and started scanning the results. Perhaps forty pages in, I found The Odyssey. At that point, five young correspondents were traveling across forty-two nations, documenting the social, cultural, and political history of the developing world. I couldn't have dreamed up a more glorious job description, and sent in my application right away, only to learn that all of the positions had been filled. The next project wouldn't start for at least a year.

For days, I paced about in an increasing state of distress. *WhatamIgoingtodo, whatamIgoingtodo, whatamIgoingtodo.* There had to be a reason life brought me back to Texas, but what could it be? Inspiration finally struck in the shower one morning: *I'll write a book!* Granted, I had never written anything longer than a newspaper article. No matter that I had zero publishing contacts. Never mind that I had no job, no car, no health insurance. I was a twenty-four-year-old with a story to tell. So I moved back in with Mom and Dad and started logging in ten- and twelve-hour days, transcribing notebooks, slugging through research, and agonizing over sentences. One year later, I had compiled a five-hundred-page tome about traveling around the Communist Bloc at the end of the millennium. Then, an agent agreed to represent it and we drew up a proposal. After photocopying it nineteen times at Kinko's, I mailed it off to New York City and took a road trip to Mexico with my parents, lighting *velas* at every church we passed along the way.

Two months later, every major publisher in the nation had rejected it. "Too bad she didn't get hijacked," one editor wrote. "Then she'd have a plot, and her story would have a point." The others agreed. My manuscript had no focus, no mystery, no tension; it was simply a collection of journalistic dispatches. What they wanted instead was a memoir; a book about me. But I didn't know enough about myself to write one.

It was a dark, dark moment. I had now lost out on Asia, love, *and* a book deal, squandering my finances in the process. I was twenty-five years old and living with my parents in Corpus Christi, Texas.

Now what?

That's when The Odyssey called, and my comadre burst into my life.

We were packing up Bertha post–slumber party at the Cowboys' cousin's home, when Daphne noticed the Kinko's box at the bottom of my suitcase. "What's that?" she asked.

"Just a book I wrote," I mumbled.

"A *what?*" she bellowed. "Give it to me!"

I tried hiding it under my laundry bag, but she wrenched it away from me, flounced into the passenger's seat, and tossed me the key. "You're driving. I'm reading."

Oh, God. I'd only brought along the manuscript because it looked so forlorn, sitting there atop my desk back in Corpus. I didn't think anyone would actually *read* it! It was five hundred pages of failure. But before I'd even pulled out of the settlement, Daphne was already laughing. "You thought you'd be 'all washed up by age twenty-five, getting plastered in the Taco Bell parking lot for fun'? Waaah!"

That was funny? Really? I kinda thought so when I wrote it, but, well, after nineteen rejections. . . .

She turned the page. "What do you mean, you don't speak Spanish?"

Aghast, I started to explain, but then she said, "Ahhhh," and I realized I didn't need to. The manuscript did it for me.

*   *   *

Thus began the most visceral experience of my fledgling writing career. Daphne read my entire manuscript as we drove the highways and byways of America. Literature has never known such an emotive reader. She laughed frequently. Uproariously. She grunted. She gasped. She sighed. She even cried, blowing her nose for good measure. And when she finished, she spoke of little else, introducing me to everyone we met as an author. *She wrote one of the best books I've ever read, soon appearing in bookstores nearest you.* Yes, it was over the top—because *she* was over the top—but I gradually allowed myself to believe it.

Ten months and forty-five thousand confidence-raising miles later, the odyssey came to an end. It was the summer of 2001 and saying goodbye to Daphne was brutal, not just because I'd sorely miss her, but because her parting words were a commandment: "You can't just let it go, Steph. You *have* to get that book out there. Promise me you'll try."

I waited until I was safely ensconced back in my childhood bedroom before lifting the manuscript from its box. I hadn't thumbed its pages in a year, and was almost afraid of what I'd find. To my relief, Daphne was right: it *was* worth salvaging. Yet those nineteen editors were also right. It lacked a point.

Suddenly, I knew what it was.

The Odyssey prided itself on assembling the most diverse documentary teams possible. Ours consisted of an Oglala Lakota Sioux, an African American, a Vietnamese American, a Taiwanese

American, and an Iranian American. One of us had a disability; another was gay. Daphne was the global citizen. And I was the Chicana—in theory, at least. My mother certainly was Mexican: Her family had migrated to this nation on horse- and burro-back from the foothills of Tamaulipas half a century ago. Yet Mom had faced so much ridicule growing up because of her Spanish accent, she decided not to pass the language on to my sister or me. Despite spending my childhood within a 150-mile radius of the Mexico border, my Spanish had never evolved beyond Tarzan Lite.

This was an issue during The Odyssey, as we were routinely invited to visit local schools, some of which requested Spanish speakers. I would dutifully join Daphne at the podium, but could only say *hola* and wave while she entertained the swarm of schoolchildren who surrounded us. Equally shameful was landing dream assignments such as tracing César Chávez's historic march from Delano to Sacramento, California, on behalf of migrant grape pickers, and having to rely upon translators for interviews. I could not speak to the people whom I supposedly represented, and it smothered me with guilt.

Rereading my manuscript with fresh eyes, I started noticing how many people I'd written about in the former Soviet Union and China who had put themselves in grave danger to uphold the very traditions I'd relinquished, such as language and religion. Like the journalists I met in Riga who had spent years in the Gulag for the crime of writing in their native Latvian, rather than Soviet Russian. Or the elderly Lithuanian in Vilnius who spent much of his twenties being tortured in prison for refusing to denounce Judaism. Or the Tibetan monk in Lhasa who shrugged off the threat of exile and smuggled copies of the

Dalai Lama's latest works into his lamasery. All had risked their lives to honor their culture, while I had abandoned my own.

How had I lost such a fundamental part of who I am?

And why had I never tried to recover it?

After sitting with these unsettling questions, I finally snatched up a pen. As I began to write, it felt as if my brain were budding new neurons and I couldn't place the words down fast enough. I performed massive reconstructive surgery on my manuscript that summer, transforming it from journalism to memoir, and implanting a new narrative thread. That autumn, I moved to New York City with a loose plan of stalking editors at cocktail parties until I convinced someone to buy it. Fortunately, my agent got to them first, and Random House made an offer. Of all my friends and family, only Daphne was unsurprised when she answered her phone one night and heard me screaming. "Of course they bought it," she said when I paused for air. "I knew they would."

The year that followed was grueling. In order to finance the writing of the final draft, I worked two day jobs and shared a Brooklyn apartment with two roommates, which meant many sleepless nights. I broke out in hives; my left eye started twitching. I flailed in doubt. Nearly drowned in insecurity. Yet Daphne kept tossing me lifelines in the form of phone calls and emails. At one point, she even arranged a weekend respite at her friend's beautiful apartment in Washington, DC.

When I finally handed in the book, I realized that—if you counted the time it took to study Russian and Mandarin and travel to all those countries—I had invested an entire decade of my life in that project. All of my energy, all of my passion, all of my anguish had been sublimated into its pages. A serious celebration was in order. I drew up a guest list and, recognizing that this milestone was equivalent to a wedding, friends as far away as Austin and Boston started buying up plane tickets. Yet the indispensable factor in the book's creation was currently stationed in Angola, West Africa. Not wanting to exclude her, I struggled over whether to tell Daphne about my party or not. When at last I did, she swore she'd be there for the next one. "Because there *will* be a next one!" she sang out.

The night of the party, I slid into a red silk dress and scattered hundreds of inked-up manuscript pages on the floor, so my friends and I could dance upon them. An hour before people started arriving, a roommate called me downstairs for a delivery. Had my parents sent flowers? I hurried down the stairs and nearly collapsed at the sight of Daphne, standing in the hallway and giggling. No joke: My comadre had crossed the equator to be there. She cohosted my party that night with true Brazilian flair, force-feeding the guests and leading us all in song and samba. At one point, she corralled my new editor into a corner. "Do you have any idea how big my friend's book is going to be?" I heard her say as I walked past. "Huge! Everest!"

When I finally crawled into bed that night, I was a joyful, weepy mess. Just like that night in the Navajo Nation.

Nine months later, I returned to my cubicle after a work meeting and found a voicemail message from my editor. "Just wanted to let you know, your books are in."

It was early February. My pub date wasn't until March 19. How could my books be in already? My heart thumping in my throat, I called her back to tell her she was mistaken.

"I am looking at a copy right now," she said. "It's beaut—"

But I was already racing out the door. I leaped off the subway at Fiftieth and ran full speed to Fifty-Fifth and Broadway, dodging hot dog vendors and florists and fanny-pack tourists along the way. When I saw my editor step out of the elevator, holding up a copy of my book, my knees buckled and I sprawled upon the floor. A security guard darted over.

"It's okay, it's okay. It's her first book," my editor explained.

They helped me to a nearby bench. At first, I couldn't even touch my book; then I couldn't let it go. I sat there, stroking it, as my editor fawned over us both. Once I regained my color, the security guard escorted me out the door. Somewhere on Broadway, I propped myself up against a wall and gave Daphne a call. As soon as I heard her voice, I completely unraveled.

"Steph, what happened? Jesus! *Tell me what's wrong.*"

When I finally choked out "I am holding my book in my hands," she started crying too. "Oh, my friend! Tell me what it looks like."

I described the colors of its cover, its weight and heft, the smell of its pages.

"And the blurbs, Steph, read me the blurbs," she said, employing the publishing vocabulary I'd taught her.

I did, noticing as she did that they were just modified versions of what she had been telling me all along.

*   *   *

Around the Bloc was the summation of my twenties, sandwiched inside a book jacket. I sacrificed everything for it: relationships (six years after the Che Guevara look-alike, I remained single), finances (don't get me started on my paltry book advance), health (hello, carpal tunnel syndrome). Not long after my thirtieth birthday, I was stepping off a stage after giving a reading when it occurred to me that I could spend the rest of my life doing this, talking about adventures I'd had in my early twenties. This is the major occupational hazard of being a memoirist: You live more in your past than in your present. It was time to move on. But where? To what?

Enter my comadre. "Go to Mexico," Daph decreed. She could already envision it: I would move back to the land of my ancestors, learn their tongue, and then write a memoir about it. "It will be perfect. You'll go from *Around the Bloc* to *Back to the Barrio*."

And that, more or less, is how my second book, *Mexican Enough*, was born: I quit my day jobs, abandoned my apartment, and commenced a new project that entailed three years of living and breathing Mexico. I handed it in, glowing with triumph, only to realize I was back in Corpus Christi, Texas, still single, still jobless, and (unless you counted my parents' house) homeless to boot. On came the gloom. Empty-nest syndrome doesn't begin to describe the loss a writer feels once her book has been submitted to a publisher. Kids, at least, will call to ask for money now and then. They'll visit for Thanksgiving. Christmas, even. But a book just vanishes. You might open the paper one morning to discover it has been pummeled by a critic, but that's it. The only antidote for the soul-ache that ensues is to start a new one, yet it can take years to conjure an idea worthy of starting that process all over again.

I called my comadre to whine about w*hatamIgoingtodonow.* As always, Daphne was doing spectacularly herself: She had fallen in love with a Quaker from Ohio and convinced him to move to northern Mozambique with her, where she directed an office of Save the Children.

"I know what you can do!" she said. "Come here."

"There?"

"Steph. You are thirty-three and living with your parents. Come here."

"But Daph. I have no money. I have no health insurance. I have no—"

"Come here. I need you."

More like, *I* needed *her.* But she knew the only way I'd go is if I thought the reverse was true.

A week before my Africa departure, I won a writing award. The *Corpus Christi Caller-Times* ran a story about it that, in retrospect, made a nice personal ad: it mentioned I was single, included a photo, and noted I was headed to Mozambique next. On the morning of my flight, I checked email one last time and found a note from a stranger who had read the article and wished to pass along a journalism contact in Maputo. "Tell him Kevin in Texas sent you," he said. I dashed him a thanks and hurried off for my plane.

I arrived in Quelimane, Mozambique, to find my comadre battling a humanitarian crisis. The Zambezi River was hemorrhaging, and Daphne was coordinating Save the Children's emergency relief operations, which meant evacuating, sheltering, and feeding tens of thousands of people. People who lacked not only cars (or buses, or bicycles, or burros), but televisions. Radios. Newspapers. Any communication outlet whatsoever, save for their own voices. At one point, Daphne sent me to a displacement camp so I could bear witness. To village chiefs dividing sixteen sacks of flour among three hundred families. To babies suckling shriveled breasts. To children, bereft of toys, batting around condoms that had been blown and tied like balloons. To women and girls afraid of relieving themselves, as there were no latrines—and they might get attacked if they peed in the forest. To men and boys afraid of fishing in the river, as it was full of crocodiles—and they might get eaten. In the midst of all that suffering, all that hardship, all that strife, stood my friend. Holding a clipboard in her hand and a megaphone at her mouth, a cell phone jingling in her pocket. Giving me a galactic injection of perspective.

Back home in Corpus, I wrote thank-you letters to everyone I encountered in Africa and, as an afterthought, sent one to Kevin-in-Texas too, as his Maputo contact had proven valuable. To my surprise, he invited me out for coffee. He turned out to be a craniofacial surgeon based in Corpus who conducted medical missions all over the globe. Translation: He was just as itinerant as me. He also had gorgeous green eyes. After nearly nine years of singledom, I had finally found someone. This probably goes without saying, but yes, my comadre took full credit.

Confession time. I don't do well when girlfriends get married. It's not that I'm envious of them finding a mate; I'm jealous of their mates finding *them*. This might just be a byproduct of having spent so much of my life as a single person reliant on friend-ships, but still. I can't help but view marriage as a loss. My loss. *What do you mean, you can't take a road trip to Austin tonight? You're going to your in-laws' in the morning? Oh. All right, so, let's go out dancing instead. What, José wants to come too? Uhhh, how about we just talk on the phone all night? What, you need to go now? Oh. Okay. Bye-bye.* In time, I stop calling altogether. I can't shake the feeling I'm interrupting something important. Like a romantic dinner. Or a heated argument. Or, let's be honest, sex.

So even though I adored Mansir-the-Quaker, I was as crushed as I was elated when Daphne called one evening with the news that they would be marrying. She softened the blow with two details, however. First, they would be wedding in Rio de Janeiro. *Yayaya!* Second, they wanted me to write and con-duct the ceremony.

"*Me?*"

"You."

And so, within sight of Sugarloaf Mountain and the mam-moth Jesus, I married my best friend and her life partner. An endless night of samba dancing and caipirinha slamming en-sued, and then two dozen of us joined them on their honeymoon on a remote tropical island. They returned to Mozambique and, a few months later, called to say they were pregnant.

All right. Gotta say it: Babies are worse than husbands. Way worse. Even the best of husbands fuck up now and then. Twice, I've flown to faraway cities to help dump the contents of an er-rant man's drawers into garbage bags and toss them into the garage with the cockroaches. Not babies though. No, babies forever gleam in their mama's eyes. Now, I *really* can never call again. I might interrupt the baby's first smile, first laugh, first speeding ticket.

A month before Daphne's due date, I flew out to Atlanta (where her parents were living) for a visit. As we settled into the car and pulled onto the highway, I felt a jolt of nostalgia. Though we had traveled many places together since The Odyssey, this was the first time we had road-tripped again, just the two of us. I was about to launch into a string of *Rememberwhen*s when I spotted Daphne's belly swelling over her seat belt and realized no, now there are three of us. Four of us. Five. *It will never be just the two of us again.*

I had mentally prepared myself for a weekend of squealing over nappies and Boppies, as I'd done with so many breeder friends before, but Daphne's bedside table featured a copy of *Methland: The Death and Life of an American Small Town* and stacks of *Newsweek*—no *What to Expect When You're Expecting* in sight. She wanted to talk politics. Culture. Art. Her life was about to change irrevocably, but she wanted to know how *I* was doing. What was my MFA program in Iowa like? What book topic would I be tackling next? (Naturally, she was full of suggestions.) The only time we really discussed motherhood was when she asked me to participate in a birthing exercise. Her doula had suggested she practice dunking her hands in ice water to build up her threshold for pain. We did this together, submerging our hands beneath the cubes and timing ourselves with a stopwatch. Staring into each other's eyes and grinning all the while.

Mansir texted as soon as Daphne went into labor. I had actually called her earlier that morning, and she was fine. Now she was enduring the most physically challenging experience of her life. Casting aside the essays I'd been grading, I started pacing around my apartment. Then my yard. Then my neighborhood. I played the CD they passed out at their wedding. Lit candles. Prayed. Continued to pace. Every time my phone buzzed, I darted for it, desperate for an update. That night, I attended a fundraiser for Haiti, where I reluctantly silenced my phone. I left early to check messages, and was devastated to find one from Mansir. "Daphne has something to tell you!" his voice rang out, jubilant. "Call us back."

I did, but got voicemail. *Christ. I missed my chance. I'll never get to talk to her again.* But five minutes later, Daphne called. She had given birth only two hours ago, but was ready to tell me all about it.

"Daphne!" I cried. "You aren't the same woman you were, last time we spoke!"

"My friend," she said grandly, "I have crossed to the other side."

She paused for a dramatic moment, then we both burst into laughter. Over the next half hour, she filled me in on every detail of the birth of her daughter—of the sweat and of the blood, of the pain and of the joy, of the "ring of fire" she crossed before the final push. She told me what Celia looked like, what Celia smelled like, how Celia felt pressed against her breast. And suddenly I could hear her just-born daughter murmuring in the background, and I began to cry. For her. For them. For us. For gratitude.

This, I believe, is what is so extraordinary about comadres. Every time you find one, it's like starting a whole new life. Daphne will probably never write a book, but because of our close friendship, she *feels* as though she has, displaying mine upon her shelf with owner's pride. I, in turn, will probably never have a child, but because of the depth of my friendship with her mother, Celia feels like a part of me. As comadres, we share our most intimate and formative life experiences so that they become each other's life experiences as well.

As a writer, I cannot overstate the vitality of such relationships in my life. In a profession rank with self-doubt, I could not keep afloat without friends like Daphne, with whom every conversation is another plank on my raft. And the fact that she has dedicated her life to international aid relief is more than a metaphor. For me, a bad day at work means a rotten review or a rejection letter. For Daphne, a bad day means a famine or a flood. I remind myself of this constantly, as a way of keeping perspective. If Daphne can relocate those evacuees, surely I can rearrange these sentences. If Daphne can feed those children, surely I can finish this essay. If Daphne can reunite that family, surely I can salvage this book.

CROCODILES
AND PLOVERS

Lorraine López

The final story in Denise Chávez's collection of short fiction titled *The Last of the Menu Girls* is a piece called "Compadre." In it, the narrating protagonist Rocio expresses bafflement at her mother's long-suffering commitment to a nonrelation who exasperates the entire family. To explain her enduring connection to this friend, Rocio's mother says, "I'm bound by the higher laws of compadrazgo, having to do with the spiritual well-being and development of one of God's creatures . . . To be a compadre is to be unrelated and yet related, and yet willingly to allow the relation-less relation absolute freedom within limits." Rocio's mother continues, articulating the hard questions she asked herself before taking on such obligation. The list of interrogatories that follow in the passage is specific to the demands made by this friend whose shoddy work habits, hapless offspring, inexplicable religious conversion, frequent transportation needs, "odd behavior," and "downright madness" would challenge any woman's constancy, no matter how determined, over the years. Yet Rocio's mother claims to have anticipated the obligations and their attendant aggravations fully beforehand. "In summary, was I willing to accept compadrazgo—a union truer than family, higher than marriage, nearest of all relationships to the balanced, supportive, benevolent universal godhead?" she asks before delivering her emphatic assessment: "Yes, yes, yes, yes. Yes, I said."

Reading these lines creates a swell of pride in my chest, much in the way that listening to the national anthem must generate a crescendo of feeling in the patriotic. I place a finger between the pages and close the book briefly to reflect on the ties binding these fictive characters and to consider the corollary for such a relationship in my own experience. The book's dark green cover is worn smooth, yet scored countless times with infinitesimal indentations, as if it were used repeatedly as a backing for notepaper. Inside, its pages are yellowed, their edges soft and frayed. I have had this book for over fifteen years. The original owner's name is a familiar black scrawl inside the flyleaf: *Judith Ortiz Cofer*. This was once her book. My own comadre handed it to me those many years ago—a gift.

One after another, books on my shelves bear that large and looping scrawl. Many are published by Arte Publico Press, Bilingual Review Press, or Floricanto—upstart independent publishers of Latino literature that mailed out copies to la Judith in the hopes that she would disseminate, review, or teach the work. Others among my books are hardcovers, a few first editions, some autographed for Judith who later dispensed them to me like prescription remedies after diagnosing problems in my own writing. A half shelf of these are books written by Judith herself: *The Latin Deli, Silent Dancing, The Year of My Revolution, The Meaning of Consuelo, An Island Like You, The Line of the Sun, Call Me Maria, Sleeping with One Eye Open, Woman in Front of the Sun, A Love Story Beginning in Spanish* . . . These are inscribed in Judith's bold script; all of them signed *Tu compañera* or simply *Love, Judith*.

The clothes I wear provide the most tangible evidence of

this enduring comadrazgo. Print skirts, knit tops, silky blouses, black and navy blazers, and floral dresses punctuate the somber hues of my closet's contents with bright flashes. This is more inheritance from Judith, from a time when I was a single mother raising two teenage children on a teaching assistant's stipend, with a clothing budget consisting of zero dollars and zero cents. No doubt surmising this from gazing on me in the same slacks and shirts day after day, mi comadre commenced bringing me heavy-duty lawn bags stuffed with clothing she had "rotated out" of her wardrobe, lovely and durable garments that I wear to this day. At that time, when we were at the University of Georgia, we would often attend events together, both of us donning "the Judith look"—a colorful skirt over boots with a knit top and dark blazer, accessorized by dangling earrings. We would sit side by side, sometimes provoking observations from others about our similar attire. "Mentor/mentee-wear," one colleague of Judith's commented. Another, a bossy pedant we both disliked, corrected this. "Mentee is *not* a word," she said. "It's mentor-wear." Judith and I exchanged a look. We knew the truth. It was, and still is, comadre-wear.

As suggested by Denise Chávez's story, comadrazgo describes symbiosis, exemplified by relationships in nature that benefit both members, such as the interaction between crocodiles and plovers, the small birds that crocodiles allow into their mouths to feed on food scraps trapped between their teeth. Just as crocodiles and plovers gain from their association, Judith and I provide resources and assistance to one another, though in ways much less disgusting. This was, of course, more evident when we lived in closer proximity to one another. For instance, in the manner that Rocio's mother fulfills transportation needs imposed upon her by compadrazgo, I, too, have driven Judith various places around Athens, but most often to and from the airport in Atlanta, a ninety-minute trip each way.

I enjoy driving, though I am neither skilled at it nor adept with maps and directions, while Judith, with her commute between her family home near Louisville, Georgia, and her condo in Athens, has no particular enthusiasm for it, and she is disinclined to leave a car parked at the airport—racking up daily fees—to drive home after a demanding stint as visiting writer, or a crowded and exhausting flight. The costly airport shuttles between Athens and Atlanta are often as packed as airplanes with tired and cranky or—worse—cheerfully verbose fellow passengers. It's much better for Judith to arrange for a ride from someone who can read the fatigue in her face, someone who will respect her need for silence. Or if she's feeling energized and chatty, it's pleasant for her to travel with a friend eager to hear about her trip; a companion who doesn't mind stopping to visit a restroom or to pick up a sandwich; a driver who, though directionally impaired, proceeds with extreme caution, if not extreme speed—yes, it was much, much better for Judith to have me to drive her.

Judith paid me fairly for these trips and treated me to refreshments when we stopped along the way. Of course, I needed the money, but beyond that I relish time spent in her company, though she was not my comadre then, in the early years of our relationship. In the very beginning, we were not even colleagues, much less friends. I was a graduate student and she was a professor. Two Latina writers of a certain age in the same department of the same Southern university during the mid-1990s—how rare was that? Such confluence alone should have been enough to forge an instant connection between us. Black-haired and dark-eyed, we stood out in sharp contrast to the others. From overhead, I imagine we appeared as striking as a pair of glossy ravens in a flock of pigeons. In addition to physical and cultural similarities, we also share a deeply rooted reticence when it comes to forming friendships. Back then, we would eye each other—silently, warily—from across auditoriums and conference rooms at literary events and departmental get-togethers. In fact, at first, I nursed a wicked grudge against my future comadre.

Before I met Judith, I had just transferred into the Master of Arts program in English at the University of Georgia, and immediately confronted the problem of having few graduate courses available in the evenings, when I was not teaching middle school. First, I met with the director of the graduate program, a supercilious academic who tried to convince me I did not need a graduate degree if I wanted to become a fiction writer. "Why, you could just hang a shingle outside your door—*creative writer*—and commence penning your novels," he'd said. He offered no helpful suggestions, so I sought out the chair of the Creative Writing Program, Jim Kilgo, who recommended I contact Judith Ortiz Cofer—on leave at the time—by mail to petition her for an independent study course in the next semester when she would return to campus. I wrote to Judith, asking about this possibility and enclosing a sample of my writing along with my letter. Her reply was swift and terse—a few short sentences, my initial glimpse of that bold signature. She did not conduct independent studies with students who had not taken at least one course with her.

I was crushed, then angry. *Selfish, selfish, selfish,* I thought. How could she—of all people—dismiss me so easily? This rejection stays with me, seared into my memory because it turned out to be such uncharacteristic behavior. Judith, I later learned, is the opposite of selfish, and years later when I attempted to use this example to show how anomalous it was when introducing Judith for a literary event, I lost the thread of my thoughts, and my telling about how she rejected my petition embarrassed Judith. On stage, she struggled to explain her reasoning, reasoning that these days I understand quite well. Though we had not yet been introduced, when she replied to my letter, Judith was already imparting a mentoring lesson to me: If you hope to succeed as a writer in academia, you need to protect your boundaries. Now that I am an associate professor who must steal time for my own writing, I am ever grateful for this early lesson, and I recognize what an extraordinary kindness it was for her to write me back so promptly while she was on leave. Still it took time for me to see that Judith's terse missive to me those days *was* my tutorial, far more instructional than the independent study I had envisioned.

After receiving Judith's refusal, I encountered her a few times on campus. We would cast sidelong glances, without approaching one another to exchange introductions. Once I ventured to a packed bookstore to listen to Judith read her poetry and prose, and I was mesmerized by the rhythm of the language, the music of her accented voice, the warmth and humor that emanated from her despite an intense and commanding presence. That night, Judith was giving me another lesson, showing me how a gifted writer shares her work, winning over even a resistant and grudge-bearing listener. After the reading I was determined to make her acquaintance formally. I planned to buy her book and to introduce myself when she inscribed it for me.

But first, some sangria to quell my jangling nerves. The bookstore staff had provided a punchbowl filled with red wine and seltzer, a few orange slices floating on the surface of this. As I ladled sangria into a plastic cup, the strap of my handbag slid off my shoulder, yanking my forearm down with the weight. The full ladle and cup, along with my purse, crashed onto the hardwood floor, the cup bouncing and then skittering across it. Silence followed the clatter, and then bookstore clerks appeared with paper towels to help me sop up the mess. In the periphery, I glimpsed Judith's expression—wide-eyed surprise that sharpened into recognition. *Oh, it's you.*

My face inflamed, I tossed the cup and paper towels into a wastebasket and edged toward the door. I didn't buy Judith's book, I didn't introduce myself. Before I slipped out I shot another glance in Judith's direction. Astonishingly, she looked up at the same moment and gave me a sympathetic smile. Shortly after that night, we began acknowledging one another—exchanging nods in the elevator, the mailroom, the hallway. Soon, we were trading greetings and then asking polite social questions. "How are you doing?" "Looking forward to the break?" "How did you like the reading?" Tentatively and unknowingly, we were auditioning for small roles in each other's lives, maybe imagining one another as friendly acquaintances. Back then, I could not have predicted a time when we would become friends, much less comadres.

After several months, I mustered the nerve to ask Judith out for coffee. I was at a crossroads—about to complete a masters and contemplating reapplying as a doctoral candidate. I wanted her advice, I told her when inviting her for coffee, but really what I wanted was her assurance that I had what it took to launch myself as a writer and an academic with just an MA, as she herself had done. Instead of offering this, as we strolled toward the Espresso Royale on Broad Street that crisp afternoon in early fall, Judith asked me about myself, about the kind of person I am. She encouraged me to interrogate my own proclivities for taking risks, and she spoke to me in a general way about them. Judith did not tell me about the many years she spent as an itinerant academic, driving hundreds of miles across Georgia each week for adjunct teaching gigs at various colleges. She did not tell me about being denied the first time she applied for a tenure-track position at the University of Georgia, about how she was turned down in favor of a white male author with a doctorate degree, a good ole boy writer and professor who would cease both writing and teaching once installed at the university, a man she would—years later—replace when his drinking ultimately cost him the position he had won out over her. I would learn all of this much, much later.

That afternoon, Judith nudged me toward a clearer understanding of myself. While I can be impulsive, even rash at times, I am no risk taker, especially when it comes to professional choices. The fact of having a family to provide for made such risk-taking all the more unthinkable for me. Careerwise, I will always hedge my bets and then, if possible, I will hedge the hedging of these bets. On that brisk walk to the coffee shop, Judith helped me see that if I must seek outside assurance of my readiness to embark on a career as an academic writer with no more than a master of arts degree and no book publications, then—of course—such a plan makes little sense. By the time we swung open the door to Espresso Royale, releasing a warm aromatic gust, I was already planning to apply for the PhD program, and though I had invited her, Judith stepped up to the counter, ordered, and then paid for our coffee.

In my second year of the graduate program at the University of Georgia, I transitioned from middle-school teacher to university instructor, teaching composition to English-as-a-Second-Language students from Europe, Asia, and Africa. I enjoyed these classes, especially for the maturity of the international students, a sharp contrast to my middle-school charges. Soon, I yearned to expand my experience teaching, and when the opportunity arose to work as a teaching assistant under Judith, I swiftly applied. I was among the three graduate students she engaged to assist her in a multicultural American literature survey. In this capacity, I attended the full lectures on Mondays and Wednesdays, and then I conducted a twenty-student seminar with my group on Fridays. The full lectures were usually led by Judith, but she had each of us present to the whole group at least once over the course of the quarter. In between the lectures and seminar meetings, the three of us would occasionally meet with Judith to plan and strategize.

Again and again, on those Mondays and Wednesdays, Judith showed me how it is done. These days, that experience reminds me of Jamaica Kincaid's short story "Girl," wherein the second-person narration instructs an adolescent listener how to comport herself properly. *This is how you address a large group,* Judith seemed to say to me from the stage of the auditorium where the whole class met. *This is how you hold their attention on a warm and drowsy afternoon. This is how you cajole, provoke, humor, alarm, and delight an audience. This is how to inflect the voice and then let it drop to a whisper before amplifying it again so eyes widen, postures shift, heads incline toward the front.*

When the course ended, Judith asked if I would be interested in assisting her with an undergraduate creative writing workshop. I leaped at the chance. Such an opportunity was the gateway to being assigned my own section of creative writing. Many among us petitioned the faculty for such a chance but few were chosen, and Judith had asked me! I ordered desk copies of the texts that same day. When these arrived, I read them cover to cover, highlighting passages in a fever of euphoric anticipation. I prepared myself over the break to critique the students' writing in objective and authoritative ways. By the first seminar meeting, I was too crammed with plans and pedagogy, too excited to speak. Fortunately, this didn't matter. Judith spoke. She was charming and witty, but scary. She terrified those undergraduates with her glossy black hair, her deep, dark eyes. To them, she must have resembled a gypsy, with her long hoop earrings and her brightly patterned skirt the color of flames, a fortune-teller who could damn their destinies in a flash. The students' voices quavered when they—one by one—gave their names. Judith, then, introduced me and herself. She talked about what she expected in the workshop, listing, at one point, her pet peeves. "You may not use the word *awesome*," she said, "unless you are staring straight into the terrible face of God." I folded my arms over my chest, gave a henchman's nod that promised consequences. The faces ringing the seminar table paled and eyes widened. In the corridor, as they shuffled out of the classroom, I overheard one say, "Wow, she's tough." Sotto voce, another added, "Kind of awesome."

After that first meeting, the workshop soon relaxed into a regular rhythm of sharing written work and critique. I labored over the stories, poems, and personal essays, annotating these drafts to indicate misplaced commas and problems with spacing, sometimes remarking on a student's infelicitous choice of font. Then I'd compose lengthy single-spaced letters of holistic commentary that invoked Chekhov, Hegel, and Aristotle in proving some young man's account of a visit with Me-Maw was so much more than a car ride to Alabama followed by sweet tea and fried chicken, and therefore, it deserved the full force of his concentrated and creative effort, not to mention correct punctuation and consistent subject-verb agreement. Judith, on the other hand, would respond to the students with no more than a word or two scrawled on the last page.

I knew from experience that she did this in the graduate workshop, too. Once she returned a story to me with the single word "diction" written at the ending. I pondered this for days. *Diction?* To be sure, my story had diction. What piece of writing lacked this? Was the diction strong or weak? Was it uneven? I scoured my draft, debating my word choices, toning many of these down and then turning up the lexical volume again. I then excised modifiers—terminating adverbs with extreme prejudice. Still, I was not satisfied. Ultimately, I retyped the entire story in plain language before scrapping it altogether. The diction *was* distracting. On the next piece I submitted to the workshop, she wrote "hoi polloi" in the margin. It was late in the term and I was too spent to launch into another exhaustive bout of scrutiny, so I chose to read this enigmatic annotation as an affirmation. Yes, hoi polloi—the many, the majority. I *had* written a group scene in the story, so kudos to me on that.

Despite this spare written commentary, Judith's observations in workshop were insightful and incisive. She could pinpoint and articulate fundamental problems with the writing in convincing and compelling ways, while I merely gave glancing consideration to these in my overwritten letters to the students. Judith also managed to see merit and promise in even the roughest drafts submitted to the workshop. On top of that, she possesses a terrific wit. Judith's laughter would spill freely, like a handful of coins flung onto the seminar table, at comments by students, and the workshop would erupt with amusement at her wry observations. "I'm somewhat troubled," she said of a story once, "by the white minivan that keeps attempting to hit the same pedestrian—the older woman, the short Latina—in this story. Think of your reader. What am *I*, for instance, supposed to make of this?" With a sweeping hand gesture, Judith indicated her petite Latina-of-a-certain-age self. The student, who'd written the story, crimsoned, but burst into laughter along with Judith. I haw-hawed, too, while thinking in a niggling way of my written critique, wherein I had deconstructed the vehicular aggression in the narrative so it reflected on multicultural ambivalence/re-sistance, comparing the white minivan to Melville's great whale and quoting Toni Morrison on whiteness and dread, while miss-ing the more obvious connection Judith had forged.

In the undergraduate workshop, students received the work returned to them by Judith, furrowing their smooth brows in puzzlement when they discovered her single-word assessments. They were again baffled, and then dismayed, when handed my heavily annotated copies of their writing along with the lengthy single-spaced letters of critique. The crocodile and the plover: Judith allowed me in to feast on bits and pieces, permitting me to refine my aesthetic while satisfying the students' need for close and detailed, if alarmingly obsessive, attention to their work. Also, in this workshop and subsequent workshops in which I as-sisted Judith, every so often she had to miss classes to meet obli-gations to the literary community at large. When she was away, I conducted the workshop, so the class was never canceled, de-spite Judith's busy travel schedule. With our arrangement, Ju-dith could board planes with full confidence that all would go smoothly in her absence, and in this way, the symbiosis—the nascent stage of our comadrazgo—commenced.

At the end of this early stage, after we had shared more than a few workshops together, Judith approached me one afternoon in the corridor of Park Hall, waving a yellow sheet of paper that flashed brightly in the shadowy hallway. "Here," she said, her voice breathless as though she had been rushing through the building, running up and down flights of stairs in search of me.

"You must submit your stories for this." She handed me the canary-colored page—a flier from Curbstone Press announcing the first Miguel Mármol Prize for a first book of fiction written in English by a Latina/o.

I skimmed the sheet, noting the $1,000 prize and book publication awarded for winning this competition, as well as the requirement to ship multiple manuscript copies by UPS. "I don't think I'm ready," I told Judith.

"Your stories," she said. "Of course, you're ready."

I considered the costs of copying the printed pages and shipping the work. I was thinking, too, of the many rejection slips I'd amassed for my stories and poems over the past few years. It was a long shot for sure, and a costly one at that.

As if she knew my thoughts, Judith said, "I don't want to hear your excuses. You will never win anything if you don't even try."

"Okay," I told her. I folded the sheet and tucked it into my bag, pretty sure I would not pursue the opportunity further. I hoped she would soon forget all about it. But Judith has a prodigious memory, her mind an encyclopedic archive of esoteric knowledge on subjects ranging from brain chemistry to folktales from around the world. Yet she can be unpredictable when it comes to follow-through, often suggesting ideas to me for advancing myself and rarely checking to find out if I'd taken her advice. Such things were on me, she likely reasoned, and out of her hands once the advice was given. Comadrazgo fosters mutual benefit, not dependency. I hoped this would turn out to be one of the times Judith would forget she had urged me toward an opportunity.

"Have you submitted for that contest?" she asked me the next week. "When are you going to pull stories together for the Mármol Prize?" Judith wanted to know just a few days after that. I assured her I would soon send in a manuscript. The third time she inquired about it, I knew I had to resolve the matter. It turned out to be easier to scrape together enough money for the copies and the shipping than to continue lying to Judith, and so I did just that.

On the day of the deadline for shipping an entry, I rushed to an office supply store to copy my manuscript and have it shipped. The copying machines proved capricious. I moved from one to another, annoying the clerk with requests for help with jams and for more paper. The UPS pick-up deadline loomed closer and closer. Finally, with minutes to go, I petitioned the same exasperated clerk to post my parcel for shipment. The store was busy, the atmosphere in the copying kiosk intensified, and tempers flared. The clerk scolded me for some misstep, and I snapped back. We quarreled before he slapped the label on my package and slammed it onto a shelf. He won't send it on time, I thought as I stomped out, blood pounding in my ears and bitter tears brimming in my eyes. At least I would not disappoint Judith and I would not have to lie to her the next time she asked me about the contest. But she never asked again.

I had to remind her about it after I received an email from the director of Curbstone Press in February of the next year. She seemed to have forgotten all about it. "What contest?" she'd said. "*I* told you about it? When was that?"

"Last fall," I told her. "Don't you remember? That yellow flier you gave me?"

She squinted at me. "Are you sure?"

I nodded. "Anyway, I wanted you to know that I heard from the Press."

"*And?*"

"I *won*, Judith. I *won*. The book will be out next year."

Judith's face grew incandescent. "Oh, my God!" She pulled me close for an embrace. "That's wonderful," she said, her voice buzzing into my hair. "I'm so proud of you." As we drew apart, she gave me a quizzical look. "But wasn't that flier green?"

Later that night, after we'd celebrated with dinner, I returned home to shuffle through the pages stacked near my computer, papers that had been ready for filing for over half a year. I spied the bright flier, and I held it toward the light—green, neon green, and not yellow at all.

Judith often pushes me toward opportunities I would ordinarily shrink from owing to expense or the time and trouble these entailed. She has encouraged me to travel for conferences in Baltimore, Austin, New Orleans, even Puerto Vallarta and Cabo San Lucas, Mexico. Judith showed me how to obtain university funding for these conferences. Each year, while I lived in Georgia, we would travel to Augusta for the annual writers' conference at Judith's undergraduate alma mater. There, we would stay at the formerly elegant Partridge Inn where we enjoyed sipping cocktails on the broad veranda and talking with whomever strolled by. We could not seem to go anywhere in Augusta without someone recognizing Judith and stopping to chat with her. I often felt like part of a small entourage.

She has a home not far from Augusta, and after the conference, she invited me to stay a few nights at the farm she and her
husband John have near Louisville. Earlier, I had asked Judith
what they raised on the farm. "Cats," she said, and I laughed,
thinking this one of her snappy answers to obvious questions.
When I arrived at the farm that steamy spring day, I discovered
that she had not been joking. Judith and John raised nothing but
cats on their farm, many of these abandoned in the countryside
and many more propagating among themselves so that nearly
every shaded place near, around, and under the house was teem-
ing with cats of all sizes and colors. John would buy multiple
fifty-pound sacks of cat food for feeding these creatures and
keep troughs filled with drinking water for them, though there
was also a large pond nearby.

My first visit, a small rust-colored tabby kitten affixed itself
like an oversized fuzzy brooch to my sweater, when I knelt for
a close look at a litter. The creature had a "defective mewer,"
Judith said, before pointing out that the kitten would open its
mouth to cry, but no sound would emanate until after a significant delay. Like an actor in a poorly dubbed foreign film, its vo-
calizing was audible only after its mouth had closed. I wore my
small cat accessory all day, rocking it on Judith's porch while we
talked that afternoon. "It's yours," Judith told me, indicating
the kitten, "if you want." Of course, I wanted the rusty creature
with the delayed mew, my warm and purring brooch. In my five
years of graduate school, my children had grown from teenag-
ers to adults, and I welcomed the idea of a new charge in my
emptying house. I remembered the aloof and low-maintenance
cats my family kept when I was young, imagining this clingy

kitten would soon grow into an independent feline given to re-treating onto a windowsill like an exquisite sculpture.

The kitten was too young to take with me after that visit, but within a few weeks, Judith brought Rusty to me in Athens. "Do you know anyone else who wants a cat?" she asked me after handing over the box. "The Mennonites dumped another litter on us." Judith often complained that her Anabaptist neighbors sent surplus abandoned cats her way. I promised to ask around. "You know," she said, "they say that two cats are really easier than one." I considered the litter-box implications of this and shook my head. She then thanked me, somewhat extravagantly, for relieving her and John of at least one cat.

Judith's effusive gratitude and her failure to mention the kit-ten's tendency to wail, mouth closed like a ventriloquist, non-stop while in a car, on top of Rusty's initial clinginess, should have all been early indicators to me that my windowsill ideal would never be realized by this transaction. With each pass-ing day, Rusty became even more social, more outspoken—if at the same time closemouthed—and more demanding in her needs for attention and affection. I would warn guests to keep their laps covered to prevent her from pouncing in them and have to shut her in the basement when service workers arrived because she would not let them alone to work. "It's not like I don't pay attention to her," I'd have to explain to visitors. "It's not like I don't pet her and play with her. I do. I *do* all the time!"

"How's Rusty?" Judith often asked me.

"Fine," I'd say, catching no more than a trace of her sly grin at the terseness of my reply. *Damn cat would probably live for-*

ever, I thought then. But Rusty lived less than a decade, and that needy feline brooch about broke my heart when she died. I wrote a story about Rusty in which I gave her white paws, and transformed her into an irritating tomcat. I called the story "Sugar Boots" and included it in my next collection of short fiction, a book that earned me a prestigious national prize. At the awards dinner in Washington, DC, I sat next to one of the judges who selected my book as a finalist, and she told me, "I can't forget that story about the cat. It moved all of us so deeply." Rusty still calling out, mouth closed, endearing herself to strangers, and of course, Judith, in giving me the small cat, had her hand in this, too.

After completing my doctoral degree at the University of Georgia, I was hired to teach composition at a women's college in Gainesville, Georgia. In August, I was thrilled to have found a position in a dwindling job market and eager to teach the four sections of composition I'd been assigned. By September, my enthusiasm dampened due to the long daily commute and the unhappy contrast between the students I'd taught at the University of Georgia and the ill-prepared, undereducated, and resentful young women at the liberal arts college, many of whom lacked even basic reading and writing skills. When October rolled around, I came closer than I had ever been to something like depression. During this time, my first grandchild was born to my daughter, a single mother who returned home to live with me so I could help her out. Between taking care of the baby and grading papers, I had no time to think about my own writing, and I could no longer accompany Judith to the garage sales we often enjoyed in the past. "Yard sailing," we called it when we would set out on Saturday mornings without any kind of plan or strategy, apart from the intention of following hand-made signs advertising these around and about the suburban streets of Athens.

"We have to get you out of that place," Judith told me, the fourth or fifth time I declined an invitation to go yard sailing with her and another friend.

I was too tired to do more than nod.

A few years earlier, Judith had been engaged as a visiting writer for a semester at Vanderbilt University in Nashville. This was a prestigious position that brought with it connections to the high-powered faculty who taught there on a permanent basis. When an opening for a fiction writer at Vanderbilt was advertised that spring, Judith encouraged me to apply. Again, I experienced that familiar feeling of hopelessness. I had nothing more to recommend me than one prize, one book published by an unknown and independent press. But Judith was adamant. "You must apply," she said. She updated her letter of recommendation for me, and she called her friends and former colleagues in Nashville on my behalf. To my amazed disbelief, I was invited for a campus visit in the fall. I was the only candidate brought to Vanderbilt to interview for the position; nevertheless I was stunned when the chair of the department called just days later to offer me the tenure-track position, teaching two courses per semester, with the opportunity to take a semester to a year of paid academic leave every four years to focus on my own writing.

When I called Judith to give her the news, she said, "I'm not surprised. You can accomplish anything, if you try."

I had to wonder—just a little—if she was speaking more about herself than about me.

The preeminent critic and scholar of Latino literature, the late Juan Bruce-Novoa, once identified me as a second-generation writer in a critical article on my work. He wrote that I am "one of the new writers privileged to study craft with a Latina mentor of established reputation, in this case Judith Ortiz Cofer." But mentoring is only one aspect of comadrazgo, and reading this, one might conclude that such a relationship is one-sided, benefiting one party more than the other. In Denise Chávez's story, Rocio's mother's compadre also seems to derive all the bonuses entailed from this connection. But that is only one perspective, the viewpoint of an aggrieved daughter complaining about the inconvenience that grates on her, just as here I am inclined to report what I can more easily apprehend—the many acts of kindness and generosity committed by my comadre for me.

If I step back from the enormousness of my gratitude to Judith, I might glimpse my small attempts at reciprocity, apart from covering her classes so she could travel. Since coming to Vanderbilt, I am better positioned to extend more benefits of comadrazgo. Years ago, I coedited a volume of critical essays on Judith's writing. Damningly, or presciently, my coeditor and I titled the work *The Medium's Burden,* and burden it has been. Despite downturns in publishing and the fact that editors shun multiauthored critical texts, we have persevered, year after year, updating the work and sending it out again and again. And just recently, we learned that our dogged efforts have paid off: Caribbean Studies Press accepted the book for publication. The first edit to the work made by the Press is the directive to change the title. Apart from this, I have written to recommend Judith for various awards and prizes. Recently, she was awarded the Governor's Award from the Georgia Humanities Council, a well-deserved and overdue honor, for which I was happy to nominate her. I teach and review her books, and I invite her for panel presentations and readings whenever I can. Yet the dynamic has not shifted: She is still the canonical Latina writer, and I remain the upstart, despite our closeness in age.

Comadrazgo, as I understood it when growing up, also describes the relationship forged when one accepts the role of a godparent. If I expand this analogy, I would have to say that Judith and I both stand witness at the baptism of one another's writing, protecting and guiding the development of this. Because of Judith, I now know that the bond between mentor and student extends long past the date a degree is conferred; that such a connection can nurture a seed that blooms into a lifelong relationship, a mutual source of support and satisfaction between teacher and student who ultimately become trusted colleagues, dear and devoted friends, and finally comadres, a commitment we both entered with hesitancy as we considered the full terms of this lifelong contract. A list of hard questions to self that we ultimately answered in the manner of Rocio's mother with a resonant and repeated single word: "Yes!"

LETTERS
FROM CUBA

Fabiola Santiago

S ometimes in my daydreams, in that quiet, safe space of med-
itation before I succumb to sleep, I return to the old neighborhood in my beloved seaside city of Matanzas, and in my
imagination, I walk the streets of my childhood. I begin on the
boulevard that wraps around the bay, General Betancourt, at
the spot where it intersects with Bar Yiya, a family hangout during my childhood despite the watering-hole name, and I walk
up the intersecting street, Levante, my street.

A lifetime later and a country away, I still call Levante my street
and the hot Caribbean sun I feel on my skin is still my sun. I make a
left turn on Pilar, at the corner where there's a house behind rows of
wild, blooming red hibiscus, and I walk past my school and past an
aunt's house to call on a friend in Reparto Cuidamar. In my dreams,
this house has a little black wrought-iron gate and a pretty garden
filled with arecas, and my best friend, Mireyita, answers the door.

"It's me," I tell her. "I'm here. I've come back home. Don't you
recognize me? Don't you remember me, Fabiola, your best friend?"

At the part where I see Mireyita's smile I fall into a deep, blissful
sleep. Mireyita was my inseparable *amiguita* during my childhood in Cuba. We started our lives together, with birthdays only

two months apart. On Saturdays, we attended *catecismo* at La Milagrosa, on Sundays we went to Mass, and we walked down the aisle to the altar together for our First Communion. We were inseparable through most of elementary school, pairing up during recess, vying to make the best grades in our class, until my parents, my little brother, and I fled the country at the start of my sixth-grade year, on a Freedom Flight on October 7, 1969.

Mireyita and I were ten years old. I didn't want to leave. I remember bits of a conversation about hiding me so that my parents could leave the island without me. I remember Mireyita counseling me against this. I was always more impulsive. She was always *una niña fina,* as my mother would say, a well-mannered good girl. I remember feeling better about leaving after Mireyita and I discussed, with that air of older girls we adopted on the subjects of fashion and boys, the possibility that in the United States I would be able to own a pair of fashionable white boots that would reach up to my knees. An improbable buy in our hermetic little island, I hung on to the thought of those boots as we said our tearful goodbyes. As a parting gift, Mireyita gave me a tiny bottle of perfume made of wood, with a beach view and the inscription "Cuba."

Para que no te olvides de mi, she told me.

She would tell me not to forget her over and over again in her letters.

I have kept the little perfume bottle with me all these years in a place of honor, among my most cherished books and portraits of my children, by my bedside. That tiny bottle was one of the few things I was able to bring with me on that flight to a new life. It would be that little bottle that would inspire me, decades later in my creative work, to divide my first novel, *Reclaiming Paris*, into chapters titled after the perfumes I have worn and loved.

During my first, sad year of exile, Mireyita and I would write each other as frequently as we could. Communication between two countries without diplomatic relations and inadequate telephone lines was difficult. The letters took so long to travel those ninety miles from Florida—three to six months, because they came through a third country, usually Mexico—that what was written was old news by the time it reached us.

But it was new to us and we had to make do.

A letter from Cuba was the highlight of our day. No matter how short, a letter brought news from home and kept us connected to loved ones. More than a letter, the words on paper were the closest thing we could hope to get to a personal visit, the closest thing to going home. Through the stories told by the letter we could return to our old way of life, we could still find a way to dream of a return.

A letter was much better than getting a yellow Western Union telegram, especially if it wasn't your birthday. A telegram was always bad news delivered in scant words:

Murió tu hermana.
Murió tu madre.

Or, days before the death, the telegram that was more merciful because the words indicated hope even as it foreshadowed death:

Grave en hospital Ramona.

Only when there was a birthday to celebrate was a telegram welcomed, even if it left you wanting more:

Felicidades en tu día.

Mireyita's letters brought the kind of news I wanted to hear, tales of our friends at school. In the letters from other friends and family, I feel a line drawn in the sand between those who stayed (the unlucky ones) and those of us who left (the lucky ones). In Mireyita's letters I only feel a shared loss. She lost her best friend. I lost mine. Our pain is equal. Those letters are my treasure, one of the few and scattered connections to a broken childhood and a homeland I barely remember. They confer immortality on my childhood, no matter the losses. They confirm who I was when political upheaval turned my world turbulent, but my life was made up of simple alliances like Mireyita's and mine.

I read and reread Mireyita's letters to retrieve the girl I once was from the fog of distant memory, from the separateness established by so many miles traveled apart in life.

"Never forget me," she writes in almost all her letters. In one envelope she sends me a formal black and white portrait. "I dedicate this photograph to my favorite friend with all my love," she writes in the back with the prettiest handwriting I've ever seen. Around the edges she writes in block letters: I BEG YOU TO KEEP THIS PHOTOGRAPH AS A MEMORY OF ME.

It is a memory of us, of who we were.

*   *   *

Girls giggling in Catechism class, girls who wanted to play the guitar and sing like the heavenly nuns, girls who thought our Canadian priest, Padre Rolando, was very good looking. Girls who played jacks. I, the neighborhood champion, only allowed myself to lose to Mireyita, who cried when she lost too many times. Isn't that what friends are for, to uplift you, to show you what you can do and be?

On our first holiday in exile, December of 1969, that year of unspeakable loss and new beginnings, Mireyita sent me a handmade Christmas card on a tiny piece of pink paper. I could tell she traced the drawing from another image of a candy cane surrounded by ornaments and a sprig from the firs of a white Christmas in northern lands.

"For my most sincere and best friend," Mireyita wrote below her drawing. "*¡Muchas felicidades!*"

I don't remember Christmas in Cuba being about those American images, and I remember how strange it felt to receive them from home. But I can see now, with adult eyes, the soft hands of my sweet friend putting her best effort into the drawing in an attempt to connect with me, to be part of the new life that, in her wistful view, would surely include a holiday with all the trimmings. Little did she know that refugee holidays are not about trimmings, but about grieving what's left behind, about remembering those left behind, about yearning for all those *Navidades* of the past, the Christmas Eve parties at home with loved ones. Little did she know that the lone doll under the hand-me-down tree makes a little girl feel grateful, but lonelier, because there is no Mireyita with whom to share the joy of a gift.

In a letter dated February 3, 1970, I learn that the Christmas card is not the first mail she has sent me since we left in October. But her first letter never arrived. She writes me again, she says, because she doesn't understand why I don't write her when she has written me twice. I write her back and explain that I have not received her letters and tuck a little gift inside the envelope.

Reading the letters that followed breaks my heart.

"Fabio," Mireyita begins a letter dated May 21, 1971, "the other day, I went to a party with the handkerchief you sent me, and everybody said, 'What a beautiful hankie! Who gave it to you?' And I said that you did, and they said, 'Fabiola! I knew she would remember you because she is your best friend.'"

She tells me, with that innocence only children are capable of, what has happened to our *grupito* of friends. "We always miss you at school, especially me, because when we go to lunch or recess, everyone pairs up but I don't have you," she says. I still cannot read this letter without tears welling. She enumerates the pairings and says that friends are getting impatient with her sadness. "Whenever we're playing jacks, I start to cry and Lourdes asks me, 'Why are you crying, Mireyita?' And I say 'Because I miss Fabiola so much. All of you have your friends, but I have no one.'"

For a lifetime, I've kept Mireyita's letters stored in a sturdy but weathered plastic bag, also a relic of the past. Originally, it held an item of clothing from my early days as a refugee child, something I don't remember, sized small, and according to the tiny white print on the plastic, from the brand "Sara Dee, the exclusive trademark of the E.S. Novelty Co. New York." To me, this bundle of letters is priceless, the kind of possession you'd flee with in a fire. At every milestone in my life—graduations, marriage, motherhood, and divorce—I've come to these letters in search of something no one else can give me. I come to find the girl who grew up by the sea in the Cuban town of Matanzas, named after the slaughter of Spaniards by clever Taínos who tricked the *conquistadores* into thinking they were helping them cross the river and drowned them. In my dreams, and despite the history then and now, it's a gentle place.

During the summer of 1970, my first in the United States, Mireyita's letters tell me that more friends had left our neighborhood: Bertha Elena and her sister, Miriam, who had been my brother's childhood girlfriend, and Lourdes, whose father was a respected doctor. I see them both in Miami. Back then, whenever anyone arrived, we visited, we reconnected if only to go our different ways: one to New Jersey, the other to Texas.

With every new departure, I can feel Mireyita getting sadder.

She asks me to send her Chiclets. Her mother asks that I ask my mother to send her sewing machine needles, N.11, because there aren't any in Cuba and she can't sew. She confesses that she's still lonely, but tries not to show it any longer for only one reason: "I'm afraid of them." Some of our common friends now hang out with a group of girls who are "*muy chusmas*." Then she tells me about the new books in Catechism class. "I hadn't been back in a long time because I was bored," Mireyita writes. "You were the only one who always kept me entertained."

In another letter she writes of food shortages with the sardonic sense of humor of an adult, uncharacteristic of her. "My friend, what you're missing! The other day in the bodega they had sweet corn, and in the butcher shop, salty pigs feet. See how well we're doing?" That would be the last letter I would receive from Mireyita. The 1970s was the most repressive decade in Cuba's contemporary history. Even having a friend in the United States was seen as a sign of dissent, of *diversionismo ideológico*. It was probably our parents who gently put an end to our girlish correspondence.

There would be almost forty years of silence between us.

Four decades after Mireyita and I last saw each other on the eve of my departure, when I had given up all hope of ever seeing her again, I receive an email from another of our Matanzas friends, Bertha Elena. She had lived for a short while in the same apartment building in Hialeah as my family, but moved to New Jersey long ago and settled there for good. She tells me that Mireyita is in Miami and wants to get in touch. I have to read her email several times to believe this: My sweet, gentle friend is here and I can see her. I can talk to her. I can visit her. I can time-travel. I can touch the past.

I wonder why she hasn't written me herself. But then it dawns on me that this is so much bigger for her. I live with memories I've embellished in my dreams. She dwells in a harsher reality. Mireyita is starting life over, from scratch, at a time when we're already supposed to be settled in middle age, when our children are marrying, when a first grandchild will be on its way soon. Life will be tough for her, I think, and immediately want to reach out and help her begin. Bertha Elena gives me Mireyita's email address, but before I write her, I go to the old stack of letters. I find her photograph and I place it in front of me as I write her an email. Mireyita writes back a couple of days later. She sends me her phone number and I call right away.

It takes seconds for us to tell each other that, despite the distance, despite the silences, despite all that we don't know about each other now, we're still those two little girls who played jacks, who went to *catecismo,* who wrote each other until circumstances made us stop. We make plans to meet, and I'm still incredulous, but I shouldn't be: Whatever was left of our generation in Cuba is leaving now, another exodus of people who want better for their children, who know that true democratic change may never come in our lifetime.

I drive out to the apartment building where Mireyita is staying with her husband's family. She's waiting for me outside and we embrace in the parking lot, my car still running. I feel as if I'm dreaming, as if soon I will wake up and this will be another daydream of my beloved Matanzas. But I know this face; the fine features framed by a perfectly coiffed hairdo with blond streaks now, staring back at me with tears in her eyes, a face as familiar as my own. I meet her daughter, who is about the same age as my middle daughter, and in her eyes I see the young women

Mireyita and I must have been when we were so far from each other. I take them to lunch at a colorful Mexican restaurant by my house, the roaming mariachis putting a festive touch on our reunion, and then I bring them to my home for many more hours of conversation and reconnection.

It occurs to me that my middle daughter, who has settled down three hundred miles from home in order to go to school, has left a closet filled with clothes that would fit Mireyita's daughter; some of them brand new and still with price tags from the retail store where my daughter worked while in high school.

I remember the happiness I felt during the first years of exile every time my mother came home from the factory with a bag full of clothes for me from a friend who had an older daughter. I dressed for many years from that *jaba* full of trendy miniskirts and pretty dresses. I give Mireyita's daughter a shopping bag and I tell her to take with her everything she likes. "Go shopping in here!" I tell her with so much joy in my heart, it might burst. Mireyita and I leave her there and head back to the family room. We talk all afternoon like the friends we are, will always be, no matter the distances.

It's been almost four years since Mireyita arrived in Miami, and one would think we don't need to write each other anymore. But we do. Our lives are hectic and the geographies in expansive Greater Miami are brutal. These days we write to each other freely via email and we post on each other's Facebook pages. I love to see how Mireyita, who was an engineer in Cuba and is a substitute teacher now, and her daughter, who has graduated from the university with a finance degree, are making their way in this country, starting anew like my parents did so long ago, well into their forties. Her own parents are gone now and she left a brother in Cuba. I wonder if exile is as sad for her as it was for me those early years, but I don't ask her.

I sense she's happy. Her emails are full of happy faces and winks. She posts photos of vacations in Marco Island and Chicago. I laugh my heart out when she writes me in her newly learned English. It's as if we're children again, playing games and delighting in each other's company. In her presence, I only feel gratitude for a friendship that has outlasted the cruelties of a long-reigning dictatorship and the silence of so many years living apart in drastically different worlds. I celebrate every milestone of her new life: She passes certification exams to become a teacher; her daughter marries; she moves into a new apartment. I watch from afar as she experiences life in the free world, and I hold in my heart high hopes for the future. I can see us soon playing together with our grandchildren as if they were living dolls, best friends, just like in our childhood. They say you can't go home again, but in the company of Mireyita, I'm always home.

CASA AMIGA
IN MEMORY OF ESTHER CHÁVEZ CANO

Teresa Rodríguez

I still remember the first time I spoke to Esther over the phone around late November, early December of 1998. She was soft-spoken and her voice had a calming and comforting effect, as if you were talking to your best friend. After she asked me who I was again, who I worked for and why I was calling, she let out a heavy sigh. It was almost as if she were filling her lungs for all she had to say. And so began a conversation that lasted for what seemed like hours. I had just read an article that a colleague left on my desk about the abduction, rape, and murder of almost three hundred young women in Ciudad Juárez, Mexico, directly across the border from El Paso, Texas.

Esther Chávez Cano was quoted throughout the article as a human rights activist who was keeping her own records on the crimes and had become a voice for the victims and their families. The more I read, the more shocked I became that such a horrific story hadn't even registered a blip on the news radar here in the United States. In the majority of cases, these victims were young women from poor families who had migrated to the border city from other parts of Mexico seeking a better life. As a result of the North American Free Trade Agreement (NAFTA), Juárez had experienced an economic boom and dozens of foreign-owned assembly plants had opened in the border city, creating a surplus of job opportunities.

For me, these atrocities symbolized the beginning of a journey that would lead me to dark and mysterious places where, ironically, I would also meet many humble and hardworking families held together by hope. For those whose daughters were still missing, they maintained faith that perhaps they had run away and were living a better life somewhere else; for those whose daughters had died, it was that same faith that allowed them to believe that perhaps their deaths had not been as painful as the severity of their wounds suggested. Maybe their attackers had drugged them, causing them to fall unconscious before the slaughter. Either way, to know that their daughters had been raped, in some cases by more than one man, and had lost both nipples—one seemingly cut off as a souvenir, the other brutally bitten off—and then were strangled with sneaker shoelaces, was too much for the souls to bear.

Yes, faith and hope ran rampant among these families searching for answers, and the common thread that held them together was one of the most inspiring women I'd ever met.

As we spoke that first time, and I crossed off another question answered on my list, I was amazed at the amount of information this woman had amassed. She could recite the name of every victim, her relatives, the location where her body had been found, who had discovered it, how she had perished, and how the news of her death had been reported in the press. She knew exactly who the police officers and state prosecutors were on the cases, and most importantly, how far the authorities had gone or failed to proceed in the investigation of each of them. This last point was what truly frustrated her: more specifically, the authorities' indifference in communicating with the families of the victims and their incompetence at gathering any further information that could possibly lead to arrests. Her passion and fury were evident. She began this fight for justice in 1993, only one year after her official retirement as an accountant.

Esther was born one of eight siblings in the northern Mexican city of Chihuahua. At the age of eighteen, she went to Guadalajara to study accounting, where she remained until 1963, when she left to work for Kraft Foods in Mexico City. Although she moved to Juárez in 1982, it would take another ten years for her to set aside her financial expertise to devote herself to another type of accountability: determining why the list of murdered women along the border kept growing without any arrests or sign of slowing down. "How come the medical examiner's reports are so complete and telling about the victims' last moments on earth and yet authorities know so little about the perpetrators? I find this very disturbing," said Esther.

I soon came to understand why some called her "an army of one." Her first offensive tactic was to gather a group of women she called *8 de Marzo,* in recognition of International Women's Day, to do something about all the bodies of women surfacing in the deserts and cotton fields outside of Juárez in 1992. They gathered information on the victims and any subsequent criminal investigation and prosecution that took place. The group was based out of her home.

Seven years later, she would launch the first crisis center for battered women and children in Juárez. "For so many years," she explained, "I have cried out on behalf of the dead that I have now decided to cry out on behalf of the living. Hopefully, their lives will not end like the hundreds of others who came before them." The center was named Casa Amiga, friendship house. It was a fitting name for a shelter, and she insisted it would not turn anyone away. I was to travel there so she could introduce me to the staff and volunteers and show me the services they provided, but first we would meet at her home.

As our news crew drove into Colonia Nogales, I spotted her two-story white stucco house in a quiet cul-de-sac. Like all the houses in Juárez's middle-class neighborhoods, her home had security bars on its doors and windows. She opened the door and welcomed us inside. I couldn't help but notice a mosaic-tile plaque next to the front door that read: *Mi casa es su casa*. My house is your house. The sentiment could not be truer. She would think nothing about clearing her calendar to accompany a child to report an incident of incest or leave her home in the middle of the night to help a woman who had been beaten by her husband. She was waiting for us with open arms and a big smile, happy to receive the journalist and cameramen from Miami that had traveled so far to meet with her. While the house was not particularly large, it was inviting, decorated in Mexican style with brown terra-cotta tiles and area rugs. The living and dining room had a lofted ceiling, the walls adorned with the works of artists who shared her kinship with the women of the world. Off to one side was her office, a converted bedroom where Esther spent most of her days. Along one wall sat her computer desk and across from it, a love seat. Inside the closet, she kept boxes filled with files upon files of news clippings, police reports, and notes on conversations she'd had with victims' friends and relatives.

My first impression of Esther was that of astonishment: This woman who could boldly denounce the authorities stood a mere five feet tall (when wearing shoes, which were no higher than an inch). She looked harmless. Her smile was warm and inviting, her eyes blue, the color of the sky, surrounded by oval-shaped metal glasses, her face framed by short, light-caramel-colored hair. She was dressed conservatively with a wool sweater, pants, and a plaid jacket; a scarf lay around her neck. She was gracious and sweet, and as is customary in Latin American culture, she quickly offered us something to drink and eat, thanking us again for reporting what was happening in Juárez and for making sure the story traveled beyond the border. She was anxious for the world to know. I could already tell that we were going to be there for a long time.

Once our cameras began rolling, her demeanor quickly changed. She fearlessly lashed out against the incompetence of the authorities, reciting a myriad of examples. Without any hesitation or concern about how she was risking her life by speaking against them, she singled out several cases where the crime scene had not been cordoned off, contaminating crucial evidence, and how according to relatives, in many instances the authorities had been disrespectful and indifferent when informing them that their daughter's body had been found in a shallow grave in the barren desert. She recalled how one poor woman had been shown a bag of bones on the floor and told bluntly: *This is what was left of your daughter.*

"Here, in this city," Esther emphasized, "it is a disgrace to be a woman and a much greater disgrace to be a poor woman." Her words would become prophetic in a place where machismo rules, where women are treated as second-class citizens, and where cor-

ruption and impunity are commonplace. Murderers and drug deal-
ers are protected by those who should enforce the law. Women, she
explained, were educated to be sexual objects for their husband's
desires, and the common belief was that if a woman was raped, she
was guilty of inciting the rapist. "If she wore miniskirts, low-cut
necklines, or flirted, she was asking for trouble, she was asking to
be raped," Esther concluded with sarcasm.

This was the type of environment she lived and worked in.
And the fact that she was a woman speaking up on behalf of other
women didn't make her tasks any easier. On the contrary, when
she demanded to know the state of an investigation, the authorities would repeat, almost recite, time and time again: "The in-
vestigations are going well." She would quickly respond, "How
can they be going well, when you wait twenty-four hours before
beginning to search for a missing girl, or when you tell the relatives that you don't have enough officers or squad cars to begin
the search or that you have too many other important cases to
work on? It is unacceptable."

Yes, Esther Chávez Cano had an agenda to stop the atrocities
and apprehend whomever was behind the brutal slayings, even
if it meant arguing with every authority standing in her way.
As Esther once told me, "There is no such thing as the perfect
crime; which leads me to believe that there have got to be very
powerful and important people involved."

Our relationship was to flourish over the next few years as I returned to Juárez on several occasions to update my stories for
Univision's Emmy Award—winning newsmagazine show *Aquí y*

Ahora. She introduced me to relatives of the victims, investigators, medical examiners, activists, and volunteers who would periodically search the desert looking for bodies. She was the catalyst for a series of reports and specials that in 2007 led to the publication of my book, *The Daughters of Juárez*, which was published in both English and Spanish and became an instant bestseller in the Spanish-speaking world. Despite our sporadic encounters, I could always count on her for any question I needed to shed light on. There was never something I had to clarify that I did not run by her first before airing a story or sending my manuscript off to my editor. She never refused to accept my phone calls regardless of how late it was or how busy she was.

Interestingly enough, Mexico never published my book, alleging that others had already been written on the topic. Although I was disappointed to hear that my labor of love, which had taken almost ten years to write, would not appear in bookstores in that country, I was not surprised. What I decided to do was send a box filled with the Spanish-language edition to a contact at our El Paso, Texas, Univision affiliate, and have him deliver the copies to Esther, as well as to the families of the other victims that I interviewed. It was the least I could do to show my appreciation for all their help in making our book a reality.

As expected, Esther immediately telephoned, excited to see the book finally come to fruition. She thanked me for giving these women a voice that would echo outside Juárez and expressed how grateful the families were to know that someone had cared enough to capture their stories and transfer them onto the pages of a book; where their daughters' voices would no longer be silenced and where their words would not be manipulated or altered. As the mother of one of the victims told me, her daughter's death was no longer in vain; by sharing her story, perhaps she could prevent another young woman from perishing in the same manner.

I wish I could have had more time with Esther on those trips. To make the most out of our short time in Juárez, my news crew and I would work from sunrise well into the late evening, leaving us little time to socialize. To complicate matters, I lived in Miami, Florida, and Esther lived over 1,500 miles away in a city reachable only via connecting flights. As it was, I was finding it difficult to balance motherhood and my career, given my two young sons and the many business trips I took. I was also somewhat guarded about traveling in Juárez. Security had become a real consideration. At least two of the people I interviewed for my book had died: One had perished under questionable circumstances while behind bars, and the other was gunned down in a ganglike shooting spree in the middle of town. In fact, during one of my last visits, I received a series of disturbing phone calls to my hotel room reminding me that I was very vulnerable and in *their* territory. Whoever *they* were. Once I returned home, I was in no hurry to go back to Juárez, despite my connection with Esther.

Though I hadn't realized we were running out of time.

In the midst of fighting for the women of Juárez, Esther had begun waging another war. I learned she was now battling cancer. Though the treatments she received made her feel weak, she downplayed her disease. Instead, she complained about getting old and not having the energy she used to have. Although this untiring warrior was key in convincing municipal, state, and federal governments to create special departments for sexual violence and femicide cases, and in changing Mexican domestic violence laws and introducing other legal reforms, a fighter till the end, she would always reiterate how much work still lay ahead. Periodically, I would receive her emails about any news she could find regarding the femicides and abuses against women and children. In one of the last emails I received from her she wrote, "Dear friend, we will always fight, that you can be sure of."

In 2008, Esther Chávez Cano was awarded Mexico's National Human Rights prize by Mexican president Felipe Calderón at the presidential palace. Upon receiving the award, in recognition of her sixteen years of defending the rights of women in Ciudad Juárez, she stated:

The women of Juárez are not just Juárez's dead. They are the world's dead, because they were killed simply because they were women. Let us all cry out: "Not one more woman assassinated, raped, or even insulted!"

On Christmas Day 2009, Esther died at her home. She was seventy-six years old. Not only did she help find a safe haven for thousands of women and children in her beloved Ciudad Juárez, but she made arrangements so that the countless hours of research she compiled over the years would also find a secure home. She donated her extensive records to New Mexico State University in Las Cruces, where they remain today. Although investigators never determined who was behind the initial killing spree of women and young girls (speculation ranged from serial killers, organized crime, people traffickers, drug smugglers, and even child pornographers), in recent years the majority of the murders have been attributed to the powerful drug cartel wars along the border, giving Juárez the disgraceful distinction of being the most violent city in the world.

Perhaps Esther knew that after her death the women of Juárez were going to continue to need the sanctuary that Casa Amiga provided, or perhaps she never envisioned that the violence would escalate to such a degree. Now, more than ever, the women and children who had no other choice but to call Juárez home would continue to have an oasis of hope in the midst of the chaos.

For many, including myself, Esther will always be a symbol of social commitment, a Comadre with a capital "C," who was ahead of her time, a leader who never thought twice about demanding change and accountability in a country that to this day has issues with women in power, a pioneer in the battle for equality and women's rights; but she was also a friend, a sister, and a mother to anyone who needed help. Eve Ensler, in a eulogy to Esther, wrote: "She gave her life for the women and girls of Juárez. She taught me about service and humility and kindness. She was a force in our movement, a leader and a beacon, and we will miss her terribly." Esther's awards and recognitions fill pages, but I'm sure she appreciated the hugs, kisses, and messages of thanks far more than any accolade.

I regret never having had the opportunity to enjoy a relaxing meal devoted to girl talk over a bottle of wine with her. Women are often drawn to each other because of their similarities or because of a mission they sense they must complete together.

We both found satisfaction in standing up for the rights of others; we were also women with voices who commanded a certain audience, and we were always on duty to make this world better. Even when it meant putting our work before our personal lives all too often. Perhaps we were dreamers so caught up in our fights that we forgot to stop and smell the roses. I believe what fueled us was the very work we were doing together, and this was precisely our bond.

I can count the friends with whom I can share my innermost thoughts and feelings on one hand. Esther and I didn't have that kind of relationship, but perhaps given a different time, place, and circumstances, we could have. But like the best of friends, I knew I could confide in her. Trust, which is crucial in our careers, is something I know she was incapable of violating. You see, a comadre is not necessarily a close friend, but a person whose example is etched in your heart. The one you'd like to emulate, that friend who gave so much of herself and asked for nothing in return.

THE
MIRANDA MANUAL

Sofia Quintero

Lesson #1: Chuck the scarcity mentality. They come for women like you. If you're not the only badass bitch in the room, that's a good thing. Don't square up. Team up.

I never wanted to cast this chick, and now she was ruining my screenplay reading of *Interstates*. The curator lobbied hard for Miss Thing even though the part called for an Afro-Latina. "With all the buzz she's getting, industry people will come to the reading to see her, and they'll hear your words."

The moment Miss Thing took the stage with a beer in hand, I should've pulled the plug even if I had to play the part myself. Instead I sat on the edge of my seat for the next hundred minutes hoping that the gatekeepers in the audience would be able to extract the promise in my writing from the slurring in her performance. At one point, my friends and family expressed solidarity by groaning loudly when Miss Thing flubbed one line past the point of forgiveness. Being halfway to squiffed, she broke out of character to yell at the audience, "Hey, I didn't write it!" That's when the teeth-sucking started.

So on a night that should have been a milestone in my nascent screenwriting career, I was feeling less than celebratory. I made my way through the crowd thanking people for coming and biting my tongue about Miss Thing's drunken inability to read the words in front of her face. The second I reached my director, who I'll call Julieta, I could see, even in the darkened café, the upset in her eyes. I immediately knew that not only was she very sorry about Miss Thing's behavior, she was sorry not to have had control over it. After all, the rest of the cast was excellent.

Because industry people, including Miss Thing (who was on to her next beer), were still within earshot, I just thanked her and said, "Let's talk tomorrow," punctuated with a resigned smile.

Catching my drift, Julieta motioned me over. "There's someone here that I want you to meet." She gestured to a woman who was seated alone against the wall near the entrance. "This is Elisha Miranda. We're in film school together, and she's an amazing screenwriter and director."

I forced a smile and held out my hand as Elisha rose to her feet. Before I could utter a clichéd greeting she said, "Girl, you got to give me a hug."

As physically affectionate as I am, I don't dole out hugs to people I have known for mere seconds just for the asking. The culturally obligatory cheek-bump is one thing, but a heartfelt *abrazote?* Those must be earned over time, if not coaxed with the purchase of a cosmopolitan.

All I knew about Elisha was that she was another Latina filmmaker—a competitor, the average insider would insist—who wanted to give me a hug when all she had experienced of me was one story that I hoped to tell. Despite Miss Thing's slurred delivery, she heard me. And in that split moment of affirmation and vulnerability, I knew all I needed to know about Elisha to embrace her, too.

"Aww . . ." I say. "Thank you so much for coming. I hope you enjoyed it despite, you know . . ." I cut my eyes at Miss Thing.

"Of course. When Julieta told me what your screenplay was about, I had to come and support you. There aren't many of us as it is, never mind Latinas, who want to explore these issues rather than play into the stereotypes."

I then notice that Elisha seems tired, and her presence at my screenplay reading acquires much more gravitas. Even if I wrote about a convicted felon who after her prison stint was obsessed with Tupac Shakur returning to the South Bronx, and Elisha wrote about a graffiti artist in the Mission, San Francisco, whose dream to be the next Frida Kahlo leads her into an abusive relationship with another woman, we both were on a mission to complicate images of *Latinadad* by exploring our differences in race, class, sexual orientation, and other identities as opposed to ignoring them. And even though I have just met her, I can tell that there's more weighing on Elisha than fatigue.

Given the circumstances, however, I only say, "It means so much that you would come all the way over here to support me when you don't know me from Eve." Elisha admits that she is feeling under the weather and must go. We exchange contact information and plan to talk the next day. This time I initiate the hug.

Our first conversation lasts for almost five hours and runs the gamut from the professional to the political to the personal. She admits that in addition to being sick the night of the reading, she'd had a fight with her partner, who was pressing her to work on the relationship when Elisha wanted it to end. I reveal that despite my show of graciousness when Miss Thing apologized for flubbing the ending (as if she hadn't been a disaster from *Fade In*), I was furious, and whine about why people like her get ahead. We dish about our experiences at Columbia, where she was getting her MFA in film, and I had done a six-year bid in the nineties.

A few months later, she meets me for lunch in the Fashion District. Elisha says, "I would love to direct the film of *Interstates*." She begins an ardent sell, assuring me that as a screenwriter herself she would respect my vision of the story, even though film is a director's medium. Halfway through her pitch, I interrupt, "I'd love for you to direct *Interstates*." Knowing by that time that she is a great writer in her own right, with no dearth of her own stories to tell, I understand the magnitude of what Elisha seems to be requesting. It's actually not a request. It's a generous offer and would be the first of many generosities Elisha would extend me over the course of our friendship.

Still, I had a condition. "Let's just agree that if at any time trying to make this movie becomes a threat to our friendship, we'll let the movie go." This is how deeply and quickly we had bonded. From the substantive conversations in our young relationship, we each became aware that the other has a multitude of stories she wishes to tell across media, from novels to films to plays. We were also aware that the friendship that we were forging was rare and required more than nurturance; it demanded protection from competition, ambition, and, later we would learn, from those for whom such a sisterhood was elusive.

"Absolutely," says Elisha. And we make a pact that remains unbroken to this day, over thirteen years later. And trust me; it has been tested from all quarters, including ourselves.

Lesson #17a: Words carry power. Waste no time in creating a database of each other's nicknames and sayings. Invent some together. The more precise, the sillier; the more it smacks of you-had-to-be-there, the better.

"I'm not Puertoricanrella."
  "La Fi has spoken."
  "That's repressed repression!"
  "E-FIIIERCE!"
  "Don't let the light skin fool you."
  "I need a fuckin' doughnut."

Lesson #17b: Never forget the circumstances that inspired them. Relive them often, preferably in front of your significant others. When they roll their eyes, giggle like schoolgirls and otherwise revel in their annoyance.

Lesson #52: Accept all gifts, especially the ones that hurt.

3222

I sit along the Seine with the Eiffel Tower behind me. Next to me sits a trade paperback of my favorite novel, *Clockers*, by Richard Price, and a marble notebook. I have a deadline and should be writing, but I can't focus. Visiting Paris has never been on my life list, and yet here I am. Only weeks earlier, Elisha called me.

"Look, you know how Ria and I go away every year, and we bought this trip to Paris?" Ria is another one of her closest friends.

"Yeah." I take the phone to the porch. It's a quintessential New York summer day with cloudless sunshine heating up the concrete and kids shrieking through open hydrants. Still, the vibrancy of the day is no match for the subtext of this conversation.

"Obviously, I can't go."

"I'm sorry."

"It's okay."

"*Bendita* Ria. She's not too happy about going alone, is she?" I want Elisha to make it to Paris. After all she has been through and all she gives to others, no one deserves this trip more than Elisha. "Are you sure you can't go?"

"I can't, but that's why I'm calling. I want you to go to Paris with Ria."

"What?"

"You've been working really hard, Sofia, and deserve a vacation, but I know money's tight."

"I don't know, Lish . . . forget about the money." No, I don't have much to spare, but that's beside the point. "How am I supposed to enjoy Paris knowing that you're supposed to be there instead of me?"

"But I want you to go. I can't do it, and the trip's already paid for. It'd make me feel better about not going if you went." I start to insist that she ask another friend to go. But I instinctually understand that the best thing I can give Elisha at that moment is gracious acceptance of her gift.

"Are you sure you can't go?"

"No, honey, I can't go."

"Okay, but it's going to be weird to be there without you." I need her to know that. Of course, she knows that, but I needed to say it.

Elisha suddenly laughs. "You know what? Every time I've tried to go to Europe, something happens." She chuckles at the thought. But as sudden as hers was, an ovariectomy is not something that just happens. "Universe be saying, *Lisha, keep your ass outta there.* You know where I really want to go? I want to go to Africa."

Taking her cue and the conversational baton, I say, "Wouldn't it be cool to take, like, one of those DNA tests, find out where you're from and go there?"

"Oh, I'd love to do that!"

"Me, too."

"We should do that together." Elisha is resolved. "One day you and I are going to Africa."

"Word." And with that settled, I pack my bags for Paris. I even dig up my college textbook and brush up on my French. Maybe I can even do some research for that Saartjie Baartman screenplay I've been stewing for a few years now.

Yet here I sit in one of the most culturally inspirational and historically rich cities in the world, reliving the events of the past month. Only days after their wedding, Elisha's husband Alex

124   SOFIA QUINTERO

called me from Mount Sinai Hospital in Manhattan. They had gone with some of her visiting relatives to see *Mamma Mia!* on Broadway when Elisha doubled over in so much pain, they rushed her to the hospital. She had known for a few years that something was not right. "I know my body," Elisha told me when yet another test showed nothing. Not one of the half dozen doctors she consulted could pinpoint the issue until it was too late.

"Elisha has tumors on her ovaries," said Alex. "It's cancer." Not only did he have to endure the excruciating wait while the doctors operated on Elisha to be sure, but once Alex knew, he would have only moments to decide whether they should remove his wife's uterus as well. If the disease had not spread to her uterus, there was a possibility—slim as it might be—that Elisha could experience pregnancy, through in vitro fertilization. Knowing his wife as he did, Alex knew that Elisha would want the doctors to leave her uterus if it appeared healthy. But there was a risk, given how long the ovarian cancer had remained undetected.

I saw Elisha right before she went into surgery. Alex stood on one side of her, stroking her hair, while I held her hand on the other. She was already groggy from the first round of anesthesia. The clinician came by and said, "Sweetie, I'm going to need you to take that out," she said, pointing toward Elisha's face.

"Huh?" came from all three of us.

"The nose ring."

And there we were like the three bears trying to remove this piece of body jewelry. First, Mama Bear tried, but the drugs were already toying with her coordination. Then Papa Bear made an effort, but his hands were too big. So Titi Bear had a turn, and lo and behold, she succeeded in removing the nose ring. That's when Elisha laughed and said the only thing I remember in those brief moments. "Now that's love."

So while in Paris, I brooded alongside the Seine, my belief that everything happens for a reason rattled to the core. *I am here because of my best friend, yet she is not here with me.* There's a ripple in the Matrix. I still have yet to figure it out. And even though I know I visited interesting places, ate some good food, and shared a few laughs with Ria, I couldn't give you specifics. I don't remember much about Paris.

Lesson #312: Bob Marley said, "The truth is, everyone is going to hurt you. You just got to find the ones worth suffering for." A friendship for the ages is not marked by the absence of difficult conversations, but by the faith, love, and compassion those conversations are undertaken. Go there.

I finally asked if we could speak, and Elisha readily agreed. We both knew that only an honest but painful conversation could navigate our friendship through the uncomfortable terrain it had reached. Each of us was juggling multiple personal challenges and a few that were even shared. So much was happening at the same time, it felt like the universe was punishing us, and like two sisters grounded and stuck with each other in the same bedroom, we began taking out our resentments and frustrations, not on our angry parent, but on each other.

There were no betrayals or putdowns, no angry emails or shouting matches, breaches of confidences or rehashing of past misdeeds. Neither of us committed a gross act of deliberate hurt against the other. Rather, we engaged in tiny yet relentless acts of thoughtlessness toward each other. The little digs, constant interruptions, and the passive listening typical of mere acquaintances that's easy to ignore. When the person is your usually mindful and considerate best friend, it hurts like hell. I caught myself shutting down, something that Elisha first brought to my attention in milder contexts. "I know when something is bothering you," she would say. "You get quiet."

Watering the seed that Elisha's loving observation planted, my last romantic partnership showed me the hard but necessary lesson of the consequences of my withdrawal. I learned that there was a radical difference between giving and taking space and emotionally disengaging with the (usually unconscious) intention of allowing the relationship to die slowly. Abandoning my loved one before she or he could abandon me did not make it any less hurtful to the people who had made a choice to love me, even if they knew me well enough to understand that I was doing it not to manipulate or punish them, but to protect myself. They deserved better.

So initiating this conversation with Elisha was a major step for me. Rather than meet at one of our typical haunts, we walked into a random restaurant on the Lower East Side. After we placed our orders, I took a deep breath and started what at the time was the most difficult and adult conversation of my life. I began by acknowledging the difficulties that Elisha was managing at the time, how hard it was for me to see her in such pain and how as her sister I was committed to doing whatever I could to support her through it.

Then I took my stand not only for myself but for our friendship. "You know I don't sweat the small stuff. That when you love people, you let them be who they are, let them have their imperfections and ride through their moments without calling out every little thing." Then I took another deep breath. "But lately I feel like I'm becoming your whipping boy, and as much as I love you, I can't be that for you."

Elisha asked me what I meant, and I gave her a few examples. The latest one had been when she recently came over to my house to plan a workshop we were cofacilitating. We had been very productive and even enjoyed some laughs. But as we were exchanging final words, Elisha uncharacteristically hushed me with a quick slash in the air with her index finger. I was so stunned I didn't say anything, but it sparked a long rumination that eventually compelled me to call Elisha to ask if we could get together and talk about the tension that had our relationship in its grip. We made plans to have dinner before another event we had planned to both attend, and I felt a little better about what was not said but understood; Elisha was as committed as I was that this conversation not be about fighting *with* each other but *for* each other.

Elisha was as shocked as I was about what she had done. Even as she remembered some of the other examples I gave, that particular one threw her for a loop. But Elisha neither denied nor questioned it and offered me a heartfelt apology. She did not make excuses for her behavior and took responsibility for the way it had hurt me. And then Elisha took her stand not only for herself but our friendship. She gently but assuredly named the ways in which I had disappointed her. They ranged from talking over her to not being consistently present when our organization was going through its trials, leaving her to manage most of the chaos. And through Elisha's stand, I did something that before our meeting had been a challenge for me in high-stakes relationships.

I listened.

I listened, I took responsibility, and I apologized. And like Elisha, when I offered explanations for my behavior, I did not fashion them as excuses. With lesser friends, these explanations can be deflections, laying the groundwork for immediate tit-for-tat or negotiating contracts that are inevitably broken not because they are entered in bad faith, but because they are created with *no* faith.

And so, through that dark period of internal threat to my friendship with Elisha, I owned up to how cowardly I had been in prior relationships. That sometimes my seemingly admirable penchant for letting the fleeting hurts slide was not about letting people be who they are, but about evading responsibility for any hurt and disappointment *I* might have caused. From the time she left my house that day to the time I began to speak at that restaurant, I repeated to myself: *If after all you've been through together and meant to each other, if you can't do this with Elisha, you won't be able to do this with anybody.*

I also learned that as much as Elisha and I inspire each other to step into our unique greatness, amplify our shared strengths, and complement each other's differences, we could just as easily overindulge each other's worst traits in the name of unconditional love. Truly unconditional love, however, takes a stand. It need not be large or harsh, but it needs to be. I discovered that it is best to free any deep bond from the responsibility of delivering all meaning in one's life. The relationship's virtues are best preserved when its limits are respected.

Lesson #479: Embrace the things you have in common including those you wish you did not.

I rarely cry, never mind in public spaces, but there I sat in the back of Via Della Pace with a day's worth of restrained tears coursing slowly toward my untouched Merlot. Elisha didn't say anything as she reached out and put her hand over mine. Her eyes said it all. As much as we had in common, as much as we had been through together over the past decade, as much as we individually were enduring that very year, this was the last thing we were supposed to have in common.

After years of relying on nonmedical forms of contraception, I found myself in a serious relationship and began using the pill again. Yet the relationship was over almost as quickly as it began, and I stopped taking the pill less than three months after I started. My usually precise cycle was never the same, although with all that I was experiencing then, it took me some time to even notice. As extroverted as I am, I don't grow close to people easily, and as much as I desire a long-term romantic partnership, I do not date much, never mind readily commit to a man. All this is to say that I deeply believed this was the relationship I had been searching for, and so when it ended, it was the most devastating breakup of my life. It became so complicated and ugly, we were not able to speak to each other, let alone salvage our friendship.

Initially, I rationalized that the missed periods were caused by my abrupt use of the pill. It had been over a decade since I had used it, and I wasn't accustomed to taking an aspirin for the occasional menstrual cramp, let alone ingesting hormones every day. Then I ceased the daily dose just when my body had gotten accustomed to it. Surely I had done a number on myself, I reasoned, and it would take some time to get back to normal.

But normal never returned. I went months without a period, something that I hadn't experienced since I was a young teen. I then blamed stress. Not only was I still getting over the breakup with the man I thought I would spend the rest of my life with (and coming to grips with the implications of the fact that we failed miserably at parting amicably), I was also facing other challenges. I was grappling with completing the second novel of a two-book deal. Elisha and I were dealing with a troublesome employee at the nonprofit organization we had cofounded. I was struggling financially while fulfilling a rewarding, albeit demanding, artistic residency over four hundred miles from home. When I wasn't making a public appearance of some kind, I was preparing for one, leaving me very little time and energy to attend to practical matters at home or in my inner life.

Things were like this for quite some time and went from bad to worse. No arena of my life—health, career, finances—went unchallenged. In more than one instance, shit got legal. Each tribulation and its subsequent lessons require its own essay, but suffice to say that far too much time had passed before I even noticed that my menstrual cycles were too few and far between. Of course, I was uninsured, but I finally made an appointment to visit my local Planned Parenthood. I couldn't even answer the question: *When was your last period?* No amount of stress could explain why my period effectively disappeared.

The woman who explained the results of the FSH tests when I returned to the clinic several weeks later said matter-of-factly, "You're perimenopausal." Only sitting in that hard plastic chair did I finally allow myself the time to register the physical changes that I had been enduring and ignoring for months. In addition to the irregular periods, I was having difficulty sleeping through the night (a symptom that I also attributed to stress). My breasts were tender more often than not, considering I was not menstruating. Eating healthily and exercising regularly was having nil impact on maintaining a comfortable weight. I finally had to accept that the hot flashes had nothing to do with the dog days of New York City's summers in a home without air conditioning. My mother was two months shy of her fortieth birthday when she had me, and I was younger than that.

Elisha had a demanding job that she loathed, and I hadn't seen her in weeks. Yet when I broke the news over the telephone, she insisted that we meet for dinner. Despite the hellishly long commute she would have to endure after being on her feet all day, Elisha wasn't going to let me tough-girl my way out of this one.

Both my hands clutched the stem of my wineglass. "It's one thing to make the decision that you don't want to have kids and to have to deal with all the backlash," I said as I released one hand to wipe my eyes with the back of it, like a little girl. "It's another thing to have the choice taken from you so young." As soon as I said it, Elisha's eyes swelled with tears of empathy. Then I remembered: I had said the same thing to her after the cancer.

Lesson #783: Shine bright without forgetting that constellations overlap.

We're waiting for dessert at Cipriani on Wall Street. Although we had been working for the National Book Foundation for several years as teaching artists in its BookUpNYC program, this is our first time at the National Book Awards annual gala. Elisha is wearing a gorgeous turquoise sheath, and I'm rocking a plum strapless gown. A week earlier we had shopped for our dresses while on a trip to Los Angeles to develop our TV show, *Sangria Street.* It had been a long time since we bought clothes together, and we savored combing the racks, finding things for each other, and suggesting accessories we already owned.

You know the earrings you wore for the Chica Luna founders' tribute? THOSE would go great with that. Wow, that's right. I forgot about those. Here, try this one on. You look great in this color.

Despite all the bustling of servers and jovial chatter of literary things, Elisha and I are quiet. I looked at her and smiled, appreciating that I could share this experience with my best friend.

Elisha suddenly asks, "Would you be willing to be a godmother again?"

"Okay, no more wine for you," I say, pulling away her wineglass.

"No, seriously," says Elisha. "And I really haven't had that much." She takes her wineglass back.

"I know. I'm just playing with you."

"I've just been thinking . . . because I know you already have two."

She refers to Alex and Justin, the children of Mylaine, my best friend from college. Over the years I have contracted and tightened my inner circle by introducing my closest friends and encouraging them to develop relationships independent of me. As I write this I realize how both fortunate and selfish I am. Not only can I name a handful of women that I can rightfully call lifelong friends, but each genuinely likes the others, which makes life heaven for me. Am I getting over like a fat rat or what? I am quite proud of the sorority I have established for myself, and I sit unapologetically in the center of my constellation knowing that each of my friends is the brightest in hers. Every woman should be so fortunate, and every woman can be.

"If I adopt a daughter," says Elisha, "her middle name is going to be Sofia."

My hand goes to my heart. "What's bringing all this on?" I already know, but I can't help but tease. She's feeling what I'm feeling. Grateful. About everything. We are blessed to be there at that moment in time, and there are better things on the horizon for both of us as individuals and as friends. The journey has been filled with gorgeous landscapes, frightening craters, and unforeseen detours, pleasant and treacherous alike. The constant through all the trials and triumphs has been our sisterly love for each other.

"I just want you to know how much I love you and appreciate you."

"I love and appreciate you, too, mama." I purse my lips and cock my head. "But isn't all of this what we've known all along?"

I am at once open to a child coming into my life in a way that evades my imagination or control, as I am at peace with the likelihood that motherhood, of any kind, may not be in the cards for me. There is only one thing I'm more certain of, aside from the fact that Elisha and Alex should and will be parents: that Titi Fi is Comadre Numero Uno. "Who's my competition? I'll kick her ass." Elisha thinks I'm joking. I'm not. I do love every one of her other closest friends, but if any of them thinks she's taking *my* job, that chick's trippin'. "I will get all *Bridesmaids* up in here."

As always, Elisha blocks my deflective humor with her relentless earnestness. It's like Wonder Woman stopping bullets with her bracelets. She simply chuckles at my edgy persona, knowing that behind it is actually a self-critical, supersensitive, and ever-evolving soul.

I now tell people I love them more easily and without expectations, appreciate all of my feelings no matter how uncomfortable, and practice more generosity with my time and wisdom because this is what Elisha has taught me. The sweet girl inside of me with so much love to give is gaining on the other outspoken rabble-rouser within. And it's pretty much Elisha's damn fault for offering her all that practice.

Elisha and I have proven to each other that it is possible to be a woman who lives at the edge of fierceness and still be loved without condition. We have been comadres from the moment we met at that screenplay reading. With or without children, comadres we remain.

MY TEACHER, MY FRIEND

Reyna Grande

I am sitting in Sandra Cisneros's dining room eating carrot cake and drinking champagne. Cisneros is so close, if I reach out my hand, I can touch her. Her home reminds me of Frida Kahlo's house with its brightly painted walls, Mexican folk art, and paintings. It feels as if I'm in another era. As if I've traveled back in time. Cisneros knows how to command the room, how to be the perfect hostess, the way I imagine Kahlo was. "More champagne?" she asks.

The next morning, I find myself in a car with Julia Álvarez. She is a thin, classy-looking lady. She asks my name, and I'm tempted to tell her my complete name, to see if she's heard of me, of my work. But I keep my vanity in check and simply say, "Reyna," and leave it at that.

After Álvarez's inspirational talk at Our Lady of the Lake University, I go to my workshop, which is being led by Helena María Viramontes. In the workshop, the first twenty pages of my memoir in progress are being critiqued. I can't wait to hear what Viramontes thought of my submission. I still can't believe I'm taking a class she is teaching! Around me are other writers, who, like me, belong to the writing community Cisneros founded in 1995—the Macondo Writers' Workshop. We go by the name Macondistas.

When Macondo is over, I leave San Antonio and fly back to

Los Angeles. There is one person I immediately call, the one person who will truly understand what this past week has meant to me—Diana.

I met Diana in the summer of 1994 when I was eighteen years old and a student at Pasadena City College. She was, and is, an English professor there. When I met Diana, I was a frightened, lonely, heartbroken girl, who had left her native Mexico in pursuit of a dream—to have a father. I'd been in the United States for nine difficult years in which I had tried not only to learn English and adjust to the American way of life, but also to get to know my father after an eight-year separation. Immigration takes a toll on everyone involved—not only the ones who leave, but the ones who stay behind. It breaks up families. It turns fathers and daughters into strangers.

I'd enrolled in an English class that was part of the requirements to transfer to a four-year college. I didn't know if I was going to make it through school. I was afraid that perhaps, just like my older sister and brother, I didn't have it in me to finish my education. But there was a part of me that wanted to prove that I could do things differently, and so I walked into Diana's classroom with fear, but also with a desire to succeed.

Diana has black hair and brown eyes. Her skin is a shade lighter than mine. And when she introduced herself to the students, and mentioned that she was Greek American, I was taken by surprise; I'd thought she was Latina. Diana speaks Greek, English, and Spanish. Hearing she could speak Spanish made me like her right away. The thought that a non-Latina took the time to learn my native tongue made an impression on me.

A couple of weeks into the summer semester, Diana assigned an expository essay about the groups we belong to (racial, economic, religious, etc.). I went home to work on it, but it proved to be a difficult assignment. *What groups do I belong to?* I had no idea. I'd never thought of myself as being part of anything outside my family. Through his beatings, my father had instilled in me the idea that I was worthless, that I didn't really belong anywhere, not even in his life.

I found myself writing about my life. I wrote as if Diana were there in my room with me, and I was telling my story to a trusted friend. I wrote how, in Mexico, my family and I had lived in poverty, so that my father left home to seek work when I was only two years old. His dream was to build us a house in Mexico, but in 1976 the peso was devalued by 58 percent, and life became much harder. A few years later, my mother followed my father north. While he and my mother were in the United States working, my siblings and I suffered all kinds of ill treatment from my father's relatives. The neighbors and our relatives used to call us *Los Huerfanitos,* the little orphans, because the United States had taken our parents away. We really did feel like orphans. The money our parents sent for our keep was spent by my grandmother on herself and my cousin, her favorite grandchild, so my siblings and I often went barefoot, dressed in rags.

While they were gone, my father left my mother for another woman and my parents' marriage ended without me ever really having had a chance to have a two-parent family. With not a single memory of my father and my mother being together, I felt cheated out of the family I longed to have. In May of 1985, my father returned to Mexico to bring my siblings and me to this country to live with him.

Our new home was in Highland Park, a predominantly Latino neighborhood of Los Angeles. We had many changes to get used to: We had to learn a new language, adjust to a new culture. And we had to get to know our father, who was a complete stranger to us. We also had to get acquainted with his new wife, the woman who had come between my parents and broken up their twelve-year marriage.

In Mexico, we had romanticized the memory of our absent father. As often happens with children who are separated from a parent, our missing father had become larger than life in our eyes. When we came to live with him, we began to see that the father we had fantasized about while in Mexico was not the father we had come to live with.

My father turned out to be an alcoholic who was quick to beat us with his belt. His alcoholism grew worse and worse through the years, culminating with an unsuccessful battle with liver cancer. When I met Diana, I was an eighteen-year-old immigrant girl battling too many emotional traumas. By then, my siblings had left home and I had no one to cling to, no one to give me strength, to protect me when my father's drinking made him lose his head. I had to deal with his physical abuse on my own. After the beating was over, there was no one to hold me while I cried. My sister and brother were gone, so I had to swallow my pain and my hurt, and feel as I had felt in Mexico—like an orphan. I often wondered if my father had lost himself during his illegal crossing into the United States. I used to fantasize that my real father—the one who loved me and cherished me—was stuck in that no-man's-land, the U.S.-Mexico border. I prayed that one day he would return.

My older sister dropped out of college and began working full-time because she wanted a car and had grown desperate to move out of my father's house. She was twenty-one and tired of our suffocating family life. The following year, my older brother dropped out of college, too. He got married at twenty and left my father's house, hungry to start a family of his own and create for himself the kind of family our parents had not been able to give us.

When I was accepted to UC Irvine, my father would not allow me to go. He said, "You're going to drop out, so why even bother going?" I was too much of a coward to fight him. Instead, I waited six months until I finally had the nerve to defy him. I enrolled at Pasadena City College in January of 1994. My decision to stand up to my father and enroll myself at PCC proved to be one of the best things I ever did. Otherwise, I would have never met Diana.

A few days after turning in my essay, Diana asked me to come to her office. It turns out that I had written about the wrong thing. "You wrote an autobiographical essay," she said. "I need you to do the essay again, but," she added, "I think you are a very good writer." Nobody had ever told me that I was a good writer. When Diana handed me back my paper, I felt different.

I had been writing in my diary ever since middle school. At first, I started to write because I wanted to learn English faster.

Every time I learned new English words, I would practice them by using them in sentences or poems. As my English became better, I began to write short stories. I was an avid reader for the same reason—to learn the language. I fell in love with books and the worlds they gave me access to. But no one had ever told me I was a good writer. No one had ever told me that I was good at anything. Period. This was the first of the many things Diana would say to me that would make a difference in my life.

When the summer ended I was sad that I was no longer going to have Diana as a teacher. So when the fall semester started, I visited her office between classes. I didn't tell her much about life at home. We talked instead about books and writing. She was always asking me about my latest story. Two weeks into the semester, I turned nineteen. For my birthday Diana gave me *The Moths and Other Stories* by Helena María Viramontes. That was the first book anyone had ever given me.

Sometimes, I wanted to tell Diana about all the problems at home, about the increasing arguments between my stepmother and my father. They fought over many things, but around that time, they were fighting over another woman. My father was cheating on my stepmother. Now, my stepmother was experiencing the same anguish and pain my mother had experienced many years before. When I returned home from school, they would be in the living room, yelling at each other. I walked right by them and headed to my bedroom. It was better if I stayed out of their way and didn't take sides.

One evening, I heard my stepmother screaming my name. I

went running to the living room, just in time to see my father shoving her onto the couch. He fell on top of her, and with his right hand on her face, pushed her head into the cushion. She struggled beneath him, unable to breathe. No matter how hard she pushed, she couldn't get him off her. I stood there, unable to move or speak. I couldn't believe he was beating her. During the nine years I had been living with my father, he had never hit my stepmother. His beatings were reserved for my siblings and me. I rushed to defend my stepmother, but I couldn't get him to stop beating her.

The fight culminated with my stepmother in the hospital.

Later that night, I was shaken awake, and when I opened my eyes, I saw a female police officer standing over me. She held a flashlight in one hand and took me into the living room, where I saw two other police officers putting handcuffs on my father. Then they walked him out the door. I followed behind them and stood on the porch and watched them make their way down the stairs. I couldn't take my eyes off the handcuffs. I couldn't believe my father was in handcuffs.

When they put him in the car, he looked up at me for a brief moment, just before the police car took him away.

The female cop told me to go back inside, and we sat in the living room. She wanted to know everything that had happened between him and my stepmother. I found that I couldn't speak. How could I tell her about the abuse? How could I tell her that I was ashamed of what he had done, as if I were just as guilty for the mere fact that I was his daughter? How could I say that even though I knew he had gotten what he deserved, I was still afraid *for* him? I didn't want anything to happen to him. I didn't want him to be in jail. *What's going to happen to him?* I wanted to ask her. *To me? To all of us?*

I went to see Diana during her office hours. I needed someone to talk to and the only person I could trust was her. I knocked on Diana's office door, and for a brief moment I'd thought about turning around and leaving. Why should I burden her with my worries? But as soon as she opened the door and said "Reynita!" in that high-pitched voice of hers, I felt that I had made the right decision. No one ever called me Reynita. Not even my own mother.

I told Diana about what had happened over the weekend. Even though I had told myself not to cry, that Diana didn't need my drama, I couldn't stop the tears. Diana grabbed my hand and said, "Reynita, you can't be in that situation any longer. You have to think about school, that's all you should worry about." We were quiet after that, and, with the tissue she handed me, I dabbed at the tears. How could I not worry? How could I escape all of this? I had nowhere to go.

"Do you want to come live with me?" Diana said.

"What?" I asked, rubbing my eyes.

"Do you want to come live with me?"

I stared at Diana not knowing what to say. I couldn't believe she was opening the door to her home. I had been fantasizing about living elsewhere, anywhere but my father's home. Except I really didn't have many options. My brother and sister had their own families and lived far from PCC, and I did not have a car. My mother and her new family lived in a tiny room on Skid Row in downtown Los Angeles. So when Diana asked me if I wanted to come live with her, my first instinct was to shout out "Yes!" but I held back, because for my entire life I had always felt as if I were a burden to whomever took me in—the last thing I wanted to be to Diana. But I knew that if I didn't take this opportunity that fate had sent my way, there might not be another.

"Yes, Diana," I said, nodding my head.

"You come live with me, Reynita," Diana said, reaching out to hold my hand. "From now on, my home will be your home."

That was the day Diana showed me what it was to have a true friend. She became my anchor. When she took me into her home, she gave me hope. Her home became my refuge.

Diana lived in a three-bedroom house across from PCC. She was from the Midwest. She'd come out to Los Angeles to teach at UCLA. Later, she left her job to get a PhD and became a self-supporting student. She had no family in Los Angeles and she had forged her way alone. She was thirty-nine when I came to live with her. I didn't know then that Diana had seen in me a resemblance to herself. A young woman trying to find her way in this big city, all alone, but with a huge desire to accomplish her goals. It was that, and the thought of me walking the dark, dangerous streets of Skid Row if I went to live with my mother, that had made Diana want to take me in.

Diana was single, and owned four dogs. One of the bedrooms had been converted into a library, but she had so many books that some of them overflowed into the living room. I had never been in a house that had books. I thought I was in heaven.

At first, I kept to the guest room and tried to stay out of

Diana's way. At my father's house I had learned to be invisible. I had learned to lock myself in my room and come out only when no one was home. But by my third night at Diana's, she poked her head into the room and asked me if I wanted to join her in the living room. I followed her out because I didn't want her to mistake my survival skills for rudeness or ingratitude. We sat in the living room. Diana graded papers, and I did my homework. During a break from grading, Diana went into her library and came back with a book. She handed it to me and said, "Here, have you read this?"

I took the book from her and read the title, *The House on Mango Street*. I shook my head. I had never heard of Sandra Cisneros. All the books I had read were books I found in the Young Adult section of the Arroyo Seco Public Library. Books like *Sweet Valley High* and *The Baby-sitters Club*. But there were no books written by Latinos in that section.

"Reynita, you have to read this book. It's wonderful," Diana said.

I grabbed the book and found a comfortable spot on the couch, where I read while Diana finished her grading. It is difficult to describe the impact the book had on me. It was absolutely exquisite. The poetic language, the beautiful images, the way the words just flowed together. But there was more to the book than Cisneros's writing talent that made reading it so overwhelming for me. When I reached the chapter titled "Sally" I broke down, and shook with an intense sadness and helplessness. This chapter is about a young girl who lives with an abusive father. Every day she rushes home after school to the house her father won't let her come out from.

Sally, do you ever wish you didn't have to go home, that your feet could just keep walking and take you far away from Mango Street, far away . . .

How did Cisneros know that this was exactly how I had felt for many years? Wishing my feet could just keep walking, keep walking to another place, to a beautiful home where I was loved and wanted. I reread the chapter and with every word I felt that Cisneros was reaching out and talking to me. I felt a connection to this author, this person, whom I had never met. Suddenly, I wanted to meet her and ask her, *How did you know? How did you know that this is how I feel?*

"Well, what do you think?" Diana asked me as she glanced at the book I was clutching tightly to my chest. But I couldn't respond. Tears were stinging my eyes, and I was unable to find the words to describe how I was feeling at that moment.

The House on Mango Street was a revelation. There were people out there who understood, who had experienced the things I was going through. This writer, Cisneros, had written about my inner yearnings. Like Sally, I also didn't belong in my father's home. And like Sally, I also wished I could laugh, and that nobody would call me crazy because I loved to dream and dream . . . I reread the book a few more times throughout the week, and as I read I began to understand why Diana said I was a writer. I hadn't been exposed to Chicano/Latino literature before. I had spent too many years reading the wrong kind of books, like *Sweet Valley High,* and those Harlequin romance novels I became addicted to in high school. I didn't even know Chicano/Latino literature existed. If I had known, I would have realized that the stories I had been writing, stories about my culture, my childhood in Mexico, my experiences as an immigrant, dealt with themes that were worthy of being written about.

After *The House on Mango Street,* Diana gave me more books that convinced me to take my writing more seriously. Having already introduced me to Viramontes and Cisneros, she gave me the works of other Latina authors, such as Isabel Allende, Julia Álvarez, and Laura Esquivel. Through them, Diana planted a seed inside me, and as I continued to read these women's books, that seed began to grow.

The months I spent with Diana were very special to me. She exposed me to things that I had never known before. She took me to Greek and Italian restaurants. She showed me foreign movies that she liked, and sometimes in the evening we would sit in her backyard and plan my future while throwing balls for her four dogs to catch.

"You have to be a writer, Reynita," she would say. "You have to transfer to a good school, Reynita." Over and over she repeated this like a chant. "If Álvarez, Cisneros, and Viramontes can publish their stories, so can you, Reynita." Eventually, she began to open up to me as well, sharing with me details of her family, her worries, her desires, her love life. But most of the time the focus of our conversation was on me, as Diana wanted to make sure that I would be okay once it was time for me to leave her home.

Diana helped me fill out scholarship applications, wrote letters of recommendation, attended scholarship breakfasts with me. She helped me polish my writing for the competitions I entered, and she was the first one to congratulate me when I won. Diana was the last person I saw before heading north to UC Santa Cruz, the school she had recommended that I transfer to.

But what I remember most about my stay with Diana was this—coming out of my room and not having someone yell at me, beat me, insult me, demean me. After nine years of receiving that kind of treatment at my father's house, I had come to believe that life was like that. Diana taught me that life could be different.

In 1999, I became the first person in my family to graduate from a university, earning my BA in creative writing and film & video. Right before the semester ended, UCSC had encouraged members of the graduating class to write an essay about a teacher who had inspired us. From the moment I went to live with Diana, I had made a promise to myself that one day I would pay her back. I saw that essay as an opportunity to do just that. My essay was selected as the winner, and Diana was flown to Santa Cruz so that she could attend my graduation. She was given the "Distinguished Teacher Award," and I was asked to give a speech about her to the graduating class of 1999.

That was twelve years ago. Since then, I have published two novels, *Across a Hundred Mountains,* which received a 2007 American Book Award, and *Dancing with Butterflies,* which won a 2010 International Latino Book Award. My third book— a memoir—was published in August 2012. Since then, I have earned an MFA in creative writing and a teaching credential.

I've gotten married. I've become a mother. Diana has been there with me through all these experiences. She has seen me become the woman I am today.

Diana is one of the few people whom I can call and talk to about my life as a writer; she is one of the few who understands me. Although my siblings are supportive, they aren't avid readers and don't know much about the world of books. Back in Mexico, my father was allowed to finish third grade before being sent to work in the fields. As soon as my mother graduated from elementary school, she was also sent to work. To this day, my mother has never read my work, and since he has passed away, my father never will.

This is why, when I return home from the Macondo Writers' Workshop, feeling inspired and thanking my lucky stars for allowing me to meet my literary heroes, I know that I can't call my family. They would say "Sandra who? Julia who?"

So I call my comadre, my mentor, my friend. My beloved Diana.

COOKING LESSONS

Daisy Martínez

The first way I remember my mami expressing that she loved me was by pulling apart a piece of freshly poached chicken from a pot of soup, blowing on it so it would cool, and placing it in my mouth. If you've ever experienced a similar gesture, you know how loved, safe, and secure it made you feel. It should come as no big surprise to anyone who knows me, therefore, that my most cherished memories involve food; from the shopping for ingredients to the preparation, and finally the culmination of serving that food to people who I love. I truly believe that feeding someone is one of the most intimate things you can do: You are continually touching, tasting, and smelling the dish that you will ultimately use to nurture the other person. I've been blessed to have had not one, but four children for whom I've been able to replicate Mami's simple act of love, and further blessed to have been able to thank my mother by honoring her with cooking of my own. Another lesson mami taught me early on is how food is such a focal point in just about any situation: a celebration, a condolence, a reconciliation, a reunion, even a seduction (I remember my abuela telling me that the way to a man's heart is through his stomach). People come together around a table to break bread, and if they are eating, they're talking, and forging relationships. As a professional chef, I am lucky enough to earn a living doing something that I love, and as a freelancer I am fortunate enough that

I can choose exactly who I cook for (I vowed long ago that I would not cook for anyone that I don't love; it would be the ultimate act of hypocrisy). My profession has also allowed me to utilize the act of cooking as a teaching tool, and not just the "how to" of a recipe, but as I cook I give motherly advice. I motivate my students to open up to me about themselves. We even offer cultural discussions. Whether I'm cooking with my children, teaching classes at New York City inner-city public schools, or giving cooking demos, I am able to fortify relationships. Teaching brings all of my strengths together, and puts me in my most happy place.

Appearing on television shows and publishing books has led me to Facebook, tweet, and blog, and I have created a website, where I have the opportunity to connect with a lot of people. It's no surprise, then, that I develop relationships with fans who frequent those platforms, and who are eager to discuss food and recipes and share their own stories.

Last year, I noticed three young women in particular who followed me in multiple social arenas, commented regularly, and even started posting pictures of the dishes they prepared. The young ladies were energetic, talented Latinas who, while they shared a love of cooking, were quite different. Mimi was a young wife and social worker. Ofelia was a student and a single mom. Rachel was a young mom and an avid blogger. Through the everyday back and forth of "liking," adding comments or posts, or whatever else you can do on a computer or a smartphone these days, I came to know these women a little better.

Soon, I was laughing with them, guiding them through simple exercises in the kitchen, and forming relationships. I looked forward to interacting with them every day. When they began showing up at several of my book signings in the fall of 2010, I decided that these were not mere fans; these lovely, empowered young women were becoming my friends.

Mimi immediately began working her way through my cookbooks and posting pictures on Facebook of the finished dishes and, quite frankly, impressing me with both her knack for food and her picture styling. Ofelia blasted my recipes on Twitter and featured them in a regular column called "Sabroso Saturdays" on her blog, *Dos Idiomas—Two Languages*. Rachel commented generously on my social pages, supported her fellow Latinas, and rigorously documented her experiences in the kitchen on her own blog, *The Digital Latina*. When I became aware of how much I looked forward to following their posts, I also started wondering what it would be like to spend a day in the kitchen with these young, bright, and energetic Latinas. Would I be overstepping boundaries? Crossing professional lines? Acting, God forbid—as my mother warned me—*imprudente*?

I decided that I would treat this adorable gaggle to a private class; it certainly felt like a wonderful way to "give back" and thank them for all of their support. So I tentatively sent them a private message through Facebook and waited, with bated breath, for their responses. While I was aware that these ladies were avid passengers on "the Good Ship Daisy," I was completely overwhelmed by the electronic version of squeals and giggles that I received from them. I threw out some dates, and we scheduled what we coined The Bold and Beautiful Blogger's Brunch on February 19, 2011, at my home. What happened next tickled me to no end; emails and posts flew fast and furious:

What do I wear?
I need to get my hair done!

I assured the girls that they were not to wear dress clothes and asked that each bring an apron, a chef's knife, and a paring knife, and, *por el amor de Dios,* to please wear comfortable shoes! I was drawing up quite a challenging menu plucked from the pages of both *Daisy's Holiday Cooking* and *Daisy: Morning, Noon and Night,* and they needed to be prepared for a good number of hours on their feet. Of course, the girls were planning to document the entire day with their cameras and in their notebooks. Rachel even asked if she could invite her friend JD Urban, a photographer and videographer who was working on a project called "Everyday People." Assured that these young women could handle a day of intense cooking, I finalized the menu.

Old-School Stuffed Mussels
Mushroom-Plantain-Stuffed Chicken Breasts with
    Mango-Bacon Gravy
Fenneled-Up Brussels Sprouts
Banana and Dulce de Leche Strudel

Needless to say, I planned for my acolytes to work for their supper, so to speak. If they were going to spend a day in the kitchen with me, I was going to make sure that they learned a couple of things.

*   *   *

The scheduled Saturday arrived and it was a cold, dismal, gray day. I got up early that morning to put together their prep trays. I would give the girls their first lesson in the kitchen: the importance of *mise-en-place,* or having all of the ingredients for their recipe on hand before they ever picked up a knife or turned on a stove. I'd printed out recipe packets for them to review, with the intention of stressing the importance of reading a recipe all the way through, and then again, before starting. Once all my trays were arranged, I tied on an apron, put on a pot of fresh coffee, and waited for my students to arrive. I didn't have to wait very long; they arrived punctually at 10:00 AM.

Between the giggles and the hugs—and the repeat of the phrase *Oh, my God, I can't believe I'm here with you!*—I tried to calm them down and assure them, with a hug, that this was nothing more than a day with their *titi* in the kitchen. Then I announced that I had planned out some semidifficult techniques for them, so that we should not waste any more time. Mimi blew her husband, John, a kiss from the door and told him she would call him to let him know what time to pick her up. I couldn't help but notice his look of sadness as he pulled away from the curb.

Once I had Mimi, Rachel, and Ofelia in the kitchen, and everyone had helped herself to a cup of coffee or a glass of water, I presented my students with their recipe packets. After I assigned them a cutting board and a station at which to work, they were asked to review the recipes and figure out how we would break down the day's tasks. It was decided that we would start out by breaking down the chickens and frenching the breasts in preparation for stuffing. This is a somewhat complicated procedure, because aside from boning the breast off the chicken with the wing attached, you need to maintain the skin on the breast intact. The same goes for the skin from the leg and thigh, which aids in the wrapping of the breast, and keeps the meat moist when browning and roasting.

The girls approached their workstations with nerves of excitement. After performing the technique on my half chicken for them, they were instructed to repeat the procedure on their own. Aside from providing them with instructions, I was there to offer advice, encouragement, and some sanitary guidelines. I stressed the importance of always keeping an antibacterial on hand for your knife and cutting board when working with poultry (beware of cross-contamination and salmonella), for example. In no time, *las muchachas* took to the kitchen like ducks to water, and I began to relax and enjoy myself, fairly convinced that nobody was going to hack off a digit or worse.

As the girls mastered their chickens (there has to be a joke in there somewhere), they moved on to the remaining tasks: making the mushroom picadillo and the sweet plantain mash and building the flavors for the gravy. They learned how to brown the bones from the chickens we had broken down, to add the aromatics that we call mirepoix (fancy term for onions, carrots, and celery), and to strain and use the enriched stock to construct the Mango-Bacon Gravy. With each recipe conquered, the girls relaxed more and more, and it wasn't long before the kitchen was filled not only with the aromas of our impending feast, but with the sounds of hilarity. Carolina, my wonderful assistant, and JD clicked their cameras in dizzying angles, while manag-

ing to never be intrusive. We moved on to the chiffonade of
the brussels sprouts, and after learning that one of my students
had never even tasted brussels sprouts before (she shall remain
nameless), she was assigned extra homework on those labor-
intensive, knife-rocking vegetables.

Afterward, I gave another short demo on how to butterfly
and pound a chicken breast, and put the components of the
stuffed breast together (mushroom picadillo and sweet plantain
mash), followed by the best way to roll and tie it up in a neat
little package. This way, the chicken would be ready to pan-
sear before roasting it in the oven, the final step. My three ap-
prentices were electric with pride at their accomplishments, and
rightfully so. I took a step back to observe the girls in action.
They interacted well with each other, stepping in to offer a hand
when another was feeling challenged. Yet, each defined her role
in the work space. One steamed the mussels. Another stood patiently whisking the béchamel sauce. And the third chopped the
aromatics for the stuffing. They seasoned, tasted, and seasoned
again, asking each other for confirmation; they toasted, stuffed,
and chilled the prepped mussels. Then they began to eye the
recipe for the Banana and Dulce de Leche Strudel, which we all
had been drooling over all day.

For those with experience in the kitchen, working with
phyllo dough is a tricky endeavor, even more problematic
for a neophyte. You run the risk of tearing or drying out the
sheets, which makes them unpliable and can lead to all kinds of
complications. So I set up two workstations for the girls to assemble the strudels we planned to bake for our dessert. Rachel
prepped the bananas. Mimi and Ofelia fretted with preparing

the damp towels, melted-butter pots, pastry brushes, parchment paper, and the baking sheets, to ensure the success of the meal's sweet finale. All this while we scrambled to find an extra pair of hands who could egg and bread the stuffed mussels in preparation for their final fry. Speaking from experience, this, perhaps, may be the most difficult aspect of executing a dinner: arranging so that all the menu's components come together at the same time, ensuring perfect serving temperatures for your delectable meal.

With the strudels already assembled, we pan-seared the chicken breasts to a golden brown on the outside and then placed them in the oven to finish roasting gently at 350 degrees. In the meantime, as the gravy simmered on the stove, we readied the canola oil to a high heat in order to fry the breaded, béchamel-coated, ham-and-mushroom-stuffed mussels that none of us could wait to sink our teeth into.

It warmed my heart to realize that the nascent relationships that had originated through social media were flowering not only before my very eyes, but entirely in my kitchen. With one eye on the clock, I managed to keep my charges on schedule, and it suddenly occurred to me to wonder what Mimi's poor husband was doing to keep himself busy on a dreary and damp Saturday afternoon. Mimi called her husband to join us; John had been banished from the kitchen to keep from getting underfoot.

Carolina set the table in anticipation of our delicious repast. I was in my zone, with an eye on each component, directing them to "check your seasonings, adjust the heat on that oil, skim the skin off of that gravy," and so on. As they managed the kitchen with ballet-like precision, I was reminded of how much I love to teach my craft, and of mami's indoctrinations of finding our joy in the room which is the soul of any home: the kitchen.

Our countdown was now in high gear. We removed the chicken breasts from the oven, drained the finished mussels on paper towels, and placed the strudels in the oven to bake while we sat down to enjoy our dinner. We gave the brussels sprouts a very gentle sauté, and in the two minutes it took to cook the sprouts, the girls shared what an absolutely unforgettable experience this had been for them, and how very privileged they felt to be given the opportunity to cook and dine in my home. It was a very emotional moment for me, one which ended in a group hug. It was then I realized that these women and I had shared an experience that would bond us for life; we had become comadres in the truest sense of the word.

It would be an understatement to say that all those hours spent in the kitchen, subjected to mouthwatering fragrances and aromas, had whetted our appetites. We'd labored without rest and without much more than a few glasses of water or a cup of coffee. However, we still had a meal to get on the table, so I admonished my new comadres to forestall the tears of joy at least until dessert! We untied the chicken breasts, sliced them, and served them with a side of the sweated, fenneled brussels sprouts, and dressed the chicken with a silky gravy that was redolent of sweet mango and salty bacon. *Mmmmmm!* We retreated to the dining room and served our crispy, creamy mussels with a delicious white wine to complement the seasoning. Then we proceeded to the stuffed roasted chicken breasts and those delicious shaved and barely cooked brussels sprouts. This was the moment that we had been preparing for all day, and as the meal ensued, we shared our stories and our desires.

Mimi and Rachel dreamed of going to cooking school one day, but were not sure that they had what it took. I looked them squarely in the eye, and I told them something that at one time I have told to each of my children. *No one ever gets to tell you that you are not smart enough, tough enough, tall enough, short enough, white enough, or brown enough. No one gets to tell you that you don't have what it takes because only you and God know what you can call upon your reserves to do, and as a young Latina, the sky is the limit.*

When the timer for the strudel rang, I excused myself from the dining room to remove it from the oven. I was struck at how these young women could have easily been my daughters, and how grateful I was to God for giving me the opportunity to inspire them in whatever small way I could to reach outside their comfort zones and explore the endless possibility that is their future. I knew beyond the shadow of a doubt that I would hold myself responsible, accountable, to these young Latinas, for as long as they would allow me, to advise them, offer a soft shoulder to cry on when necessary, and cuff their collars when I thought that was what they needed. Though I would continue to monitor their growth through our social media outlets, they now had my cell phone number and my address, and I would encourage them to use both without reservation.

I plated the strudel, drizzled some dulce de leche over the flaky banana treat, and attempted to swallow the knot of emotion that had formed in my throat. As I served the last course, I knew that while our meal was approaching its end, it marked the beginning of long and meaningful relationships; and I understood that bonds like these could only truly be shared among women.

After cleaning up—more tears, more hugs, and promises to share pictures and blog links—I prepared care packages for the girls, like any good comadre would, walked them to the door, and secured buttons and warm scarves against the cold weather. In the days to come, I caught myself smiling, remembering a funny line or anecdote that we had shared together. And then I was completely blown away when not just Mimi, but Rachel as well, let me know they had made appointments to tour my alma mater, the French Culinary Institute in Manhattan. I made it a point to be available to them whenever I thought they needed a shot in the arm or a dose of moral support. Our Saturday in the kitchen, which started out as a gesture of appreciation for three young women who had showered me with their support, turned into a life lesson:

You never know who is watching you for inspiration. It's always better to be on your best behavior, so that the lessons you teach by example are positive.

On November 1, 2011, I attended Mimi's graduation from the French Culinary Institute. She'd quit her job as a social worker, and while scared out of her mind, dove into the culinary arena headfirst. Rachel is working as a bilingual paralegal full time these days, but says her passion for food never ceases to be a huge part of her everyday life. Ofelia is wrapping up her academic pursuits and is planning her wedding this year. Me, I continue to be proud of my comadres and their accomplishments. You know *how* I know? At the FCI ceremony, I was that woman in the front row, with the cheerleading pom-poms, and the ridiculously large grin pasted on her face, jumping up and down with excitement. I am their comadre.

ANARCHY CHICKS

Michelle Herrera Mulligan

When Ms. Litz* introduced Tara Nelsen to our second-grade class, I didn't notice. I'd been too distracted watching the clock. The goon squad was scheduled to come for me at 10:00 AM. I was short of time.

After my parents announced their divorce, I went from mealy mouthed shy to near mute, and Ms. Litz recommended I visit the school therapist. I dreaded the appointment. I'd seen "Dr. Ann" before. She sat in an airless office near the lunchroom, a hole where Mexicans and foster kids disappeared for hours.

Dr. Ann arrived with her assistant at 10:02 AM. They waited patiently behind the door, while Ms. Litz called my name. I was probably looking down as I headed to the front, passing the desk where the new girl sat.

When we got to her office, Dr. Ann sat me in front of a small table. She glanced at her assistant, who quickly left the room.

"So I thought we could play a little game . . . wouldn't that be fun?" she started.

"What kind of game?" I said.

"Well, maybe we could pretend you are at home."

She placed a large collapsible dollhouse on top of the desk. To open it, you had to fold it out at the center. Aside from the

* All names, except for Tara's and the author's, have been changed.

confidence-inspiring pink paint on the roof, the rooms were large and undecorated.

"Look," Dr. Ann said, as she put a toy velvet couch and a few faceless dolls in the center. "Why don't you show me how things are in your house?"

I didn't understand.

"Do you want the happy house or the sad house?" I asked.

"What's the difference?"

I shrugged. In the happy house, the couch would tip over. There were not enough dolls to represent the chaos of my brothers, parents, *tios,* and *abuelita* in the same room, or the *cumbias* and throaty laughs that came with them.

"Why don't you show me the sad house?"

I didn't answer. After she moved out, my mother started coming by for a few hours after school every day. The sad house was the one she left behind, as empty as a carcass open before me. How could I describe my father, brothers, and myself sitting tensely on velvet, holding frozen-pizza-stained paper plates, and trying not to notice the gap forming between us?

"I don't want to talk. I want to go back to class," I said.

"Okay," she said, closing up the house. "That's enough for today."

But I knew the therapy wasn't over. I had to start speaking up, or I would be trapped in front of the dollhouse soon enough.

The lunch bell rang as I left Dr. Ann's office. I found my class just as they were lining up outside of the door of the lunchroom. Chip Salders covered his mouth, as if to stifle a loud snort, when I passed him. "Hey, it's the psycho!"

Sandy Marstead, who was last in line, jumped as I took my place behind her. "Ms. Litz, she's *touching* me again." I took a few steps back. I waited while everyone else filed into the cafeteria. I was stalling, kicking my shoes against the wall, when I first heard Tara's voice.

"Hey, are you coming?"

"What?" I was sure she was talking to someone else. I turned around. Her hair was womanly long: wild, honey-blond, and halfway down her back. There were no bangs, barrettes, or other signs of little-girldom to blunt the effect. A plastic headband revealed a pair of wide hazel-brown eyes on a thin, heart-shaped face.

"Can't you talk? Are you coming to lunch or what?" she asked, with a little smile. She had buckteeth, but she didn't hide them. She smiled wider.

"Yeah, I was just about to . . ." I mumbled. Tara rolled her eyes.

"Well, come on then." She grabbed me by the sleeve and dragged me with her.

When we walked into our small, crowded lunchroom, I tried to slip away. I was used to sitting alone in my corner with my face buried in an aluminum-wrapped ham and cheese and my shriveled copy of *The Phantom Tollbooth*. My back was already turned from her when she caught my arm again.

"Don't you want to sit together? Jeez."

"No, well, yeah, I just thought . . ."

"Just sit down already." With a tug, I was on the bench.

"What's your name?"

"Michy," I whispered. It was embarrassing, but true.

"Fishy?"

"No, MICHy."

"Oh, well I'm TAH-RA, not Tara, like the house in that book," she said.

"Is that sandwich really just jelly?" I asked, in horror, as I watched her bite into a Wonder bread and grape concoction.

"Are you *really* going to read that book?" she said, as she saw me open my wrinkled paperback, crushing Milo's face behind the seam for the thousandth time.

Neither of us answered, in awe of each other's weirdness.

"Do you want to come to my house after school?"

"Do you always talk so loud?" I asked.

"C'monnnnn . . . we can walk together, I know the way now; I can get there all by myself." She poked me in the side quickly with her index finger, as if to shake me out of my stubbornness.

"I can't, ummm, I have to ask my ma . . . I mean my dad . . . I don't know who'll be home."

My mouth twisted over invisible marbles. Nobody talked about where mami was living, but it seemed shadowy, unfathomable to me at the time.

"So?" She shrugged. "My mom's never there either. She's at work."

I watched her quietly as she finished her sandwich. Her sweet voice didn't fit her thin, wiry body. She looked small but tough, a brawler in boy's clothing.

Tara had moved to Carpentersville, Illinois, after her mother had come home one day and announced that she'd gotten married. They would be moving from their apartment behind the

Venture discount mart to a house on a tree-lined street. Tara had met her new stepdad, a roly-poly man with stringy hair and a thick beard, once. Her mother said he had arranged everything. It was her first week in town. From the moment she saw me in that line, we became a unit, a blend of soft grain and hard stalk that combined quickly in order to survive.

Soon after, she began climbing up trees with me at lunchtime so we could read books, which I supplied in bulk. We checked in with each other via passed notes or across-the-room eye rolls every fifteen minutes. We plotted against our enemies, signed to each other in code, and tracked the every movement of our latest crush. If someone took a shot at me, I stuttered, and she sucker-punched. She glared. She swung her strong shoulders with force. She was like the sister I had always dreamed of, only tougher, funnier, and smarter.

"Where'd you get those pants?" they'd ask.

"The same place your mom got that slutty tube top."

"Why are you with that retard?"

"Why are you so ugly?" She spoke their poverty punk.

Ms. "Hasnotits" often threatened detention. Chip "Snot-nose" and Sandy "Smellsbad" now stepped in line without comment. Ms. Litz eventually separated us in class, but at least there was no more talk of therapy. Under her influence, my words came quicker.

"You want to come over?" Tara asked, almost every day, without worrying about why my mother didn't like her. "Just come to my house, after school."

"I can't."

"Why not?"

"Because my mom . . ."

"So what? Just do it anyway."

The first day I snuck over, it was warm inside, the walls crackling with fake wood paneling and the smell of cigarettes. She stood on a pile of books and started up the stove.

"What are you doing?"

"I'm making dinner."

"But I'm supposed to be home at four . . ."

"Who cares?"

She waited for the water to boil, and then added the flavor packet and noodles from a box of macaroni and cheese. "I don't like the milk," she said. "So it's just gonna be butter." Later, we played animal hospital, replacing the stitching of her torn teddy bears with masking tape and covering bruised eyes with paper bandages. "What happened, anyway? With your mom and dad? How come she don't live there?"

"I think she hates him."

"Oh." she nodded. "How come?"

"I don't know, but she's trying to come back. She wants him to live somewhere else." I turned the stuffed animals over, piling them up as if ready for their body bags.

"It's okay, you can come here," she said, letting her hand brush my shoulder as she picked up a worn panda. "Whenever you want, okay? It's just you and me."

"But I don't know where we'll be," I said, my eyes starting to fill. I yanked the panda back, slowly twisting his ears out of their recent stitching. "My daddy says he doesn't want to move out."

"You'll be here," she interrupted, gently taking him out of

my hand. "You can just come over." She placed the bear high on the bed. He was a leper miraculously healed, his plastic eyes turned upward as if to face the light.

By fifth grade, the line erased between her family and my own. My mother had won back custody and was slowly making her way back into my house. As conciliation for the brutality of their divorce, both of my parents now accepted Tara. The hours from three to five belonged to her, and to the vast woods that spread wildly around our houses. My mother nicknamed her Taralecas and once shoved a spicy peanut powder from the Mexican grocery into her mouth, the way a tigress would force-feed a runt, laughing hysterically while Tara coughed, and tears poured down her face.

My father even allowed me to bring her along on some of our awkward post-divorce dates. When I first saw him waiting for us in a loud bowling alley, I noticed that his signature rugby shirts looked too big and bright, as if no one were there to tell him he'd bought the wrong one. Whenever the miniature golf speed rounds got too competitive, or the tinny disco remixes at the bowling alley became overwhelming, Tara knew how to keep us both distracted.

On the days Tara's stepfather drove us to school in his pick-up truck, I learned the words to "The Devil Went Down to Georgia," which seemed to be stuck on an endless loop on his battered eight-track. I remembered not to put my feet on the cloth that covered the hole on the passenger's floorboard.

Her mother called me hon, and when I wanted to spend the

night, sometimes Tara had to call the local bars to find her and ask permission.

"Sure, what the hell?" I heard her deep voice on the phone. "Maybe she'll help keep you from burning the place down."

We had different games as the years passed. If there was no money for the bus, we stayed in her room and made bets on the outfits her neighbors would wear to church. We made prank calls and rang doorbells. With no adults around, it was like our own little permanent frat party. We held séances and asked the Ouija board for advice. Barbie went from PTA mom to a home wrecker. Skipper was a runaway down on her luck, forced to work as a teen prostitute when she wasn't practicing for her all-girl rock band.

Nothing belonged to either one of us. She took gum out of my mouth and answered questions directed at me in class. "How did you know I wasn't paying attention?" I asked her once. "Duh," she said. "I could feel your head traveling toward space from across the room." One afternoon, a teacher called me aside to ask if I wanted to try ESL classes. They asked every year, even though I had an Irishman's last name and only spoke Spanish *cuando quería Taco Bell*. Tara overheard.

"Why do they act like you're Mexican, 'cause your family is?" She looked me up and down suspiciously, as if I'd been an imposter all along. "Did you *ever* speak Spanish? How come your English is so good then?"

"Nah, it's not even all of my family," I said, nervously. "Just my mom's side. I can't really speak Spanish anyway."

"So you're not Mexican, just your mom's family?"

I didn't want to be Mexican. I didn't like the way the dads

drove trucks that blasted loud, twangy accordion music that made my ears hurt or how the moms always smelled like onion when they left the kitchen.

"Yeah," I said, relieved. "That's right."

That year, our school decided to have an afternoon Halloween parade in the neighborhood. My mother said she'd surprise me with my costume. On the morning of the big day, I came out of my bedroom to find a grotesque hooked-nosed witch mask sitting on the couch like a severed head. My mother was sitting cozily next to it like a friend invited to tea. "Don't you love it!" she said. "I went to every store in the mall to find something different, you know? I'll make you' nails long and pain' dem so dey look real scary. No one is going to be like you." Ever a lover of the macabre, I paired the mask with a black cape and a short pink skirt.

I was nervous about how the kids at school would react, but I didn't want to disappoint her. The mask's designer didn't seem to account for air holes, so by the time I got to school I was breathless and sweaty. Everyone stared as I walked by. In our classroom's yellow light, it had an even more disturbing quality, as if the hags of *Macbeth* had caught a bad case of diphtheria. The stares devolved into whispers, and everyone seemed transfixed on my deathly pallor. After an hour, it was too much. I excused myself the first chance I got and went running to the bathroom. Tara quickly followed and found me crying off the green makeup my mother had added for authenticity on my cheeks and neck.

"Why are *you* crying?" she asked, stunned.

"Everyone's looking at me. I feel weird."

"You feel weird?" She dramatically slid her own plastic mask over her face. "Look at me! I'm a freakin' Ewok." The oversized molded cheeks meant to simulate *Return of the Jedi*'s little pockets of cheer didn't even cover her face. "At least your mother tried to find something. I think mine just bought this at the dollar store, five minutes before I had to leave!" she said, shifting uncomfortably under the black plastic that formed the rest of her costume. "If you want, I'll wear the freakin' thing."

She held her hand out and looked at me. I can't remember if she wore it for a while, and hammed it up at the parade, chasing little kids and shouting her curses, or if I just imagined that she did whenever I needed a laugh. Either way, after that I was fine. By the time my mother arrived, I had the mask and a fresh layer of makeup on, the tears long dried off my face.

Tara could be moody. Sometimes I wouldn't find a note on my chair when I got to school. On those days, no matter how often I said her name, she wouldn't turn around. When I got to the lunchroom, she would already be gone. She had turned eleven, and at recess she would go on walks around the playground with boys or hang out with girls who liked to ride bikes or play different. I climbed the tree myself. Or swung as high as I could go. I waited. One way or another, she always came back.

One autumn morning, she came to school with a slightly rusted razor blade she found in her stepdad's cabinet. At recess, we climbed the big hill, past the part where the grass turned brown and the rubber tire hung from the tree.

"We're going to be blood sisters, okay?" she said. "Just

hold out your finger, it's not going to hurt that bad." As usual, I didn't say much. I just closed my eyes and stretched out my arm, waiting for the heat of her hand against my own.

When elementary school ended, and it was finally time for us to change districts for our junior high, Tara decided we needed a makeover. We were going to be joining the rich kids in Barrington, and we had to look good. A week or two before classes started, we headed to the mall. We dug through the clearance racks of novelty stores and tween standbys, looking for an outfit or two we could buy with our babysitting money.

Tara gave up the tomboy look and decided to experiment with blue eye shadow and short rocker skirts. We played George Michael songs and did Duran Duran dance numbers and tried on endless combinations of asymmetrical skirts, neon tanks, and other gems found in the clearance bin. In the mirror, we recounted our defects for the thousandth time.

On the first day of school, I was on my own for at least the first few hours before lunch. Tara and I weren't in the same classes. The school looked huge, clean, almost like an amphitheater compared to the small, cramped classrooms at our elementary school.

By third period, my stomach was shredded: It was time for gym, and I was on my own. No Tara to hide behind. By the time the class was over, I was a nervous wreck. I ran back into the hot locker room, my hands reeking of sweat and Jean Naté, rushing to put my outfit back on. I was trying to remember where the mirrors were, so I could reinforce my pink lip gloss, when I heard the smooth voices behind me.

"Hey, what's the difference between a spic and a hooker?"

"A spic *smells* like trash and is too stupid to charge." I heard giggles, coming closer.

"Do you see what she's *wearing?*"

I felt an evil thrill rush through me as I finished pulling on my jeans and my shirt. It was mean, but they must have been talking about the Martínez sisters, *cholas*-in-training who used to throw rocks and pick fights with all the girls on my block. The voices behind me had to belong to the Real White Girls I had just seen walking into the locker room. They were late-eighties perfect, decked out in Guess jeans and crisp, ironed $150 shirts, their oiled curls permed by professionals. They were extra qualified to put trash in its place. I wanted to join in. Until I slowly turned and realized that there wasn't anyone else in the room besides me.

"Well, aren't you going to say anything, little girl? Or do you not *habla inglés?*"

I stood trembling until they left, unable to get my books into my bag and myself out the door. I couldn't wait until I saw Tara to let her know what had happened. She would fix things; she would know what to say. But when I did see her at lunch, she was laughing, looking around the pastel-colored cafeteria like an explorer crossing a new mountain. "It's so cool here, right?" she said, her attention fixed on everyone passing by the table where we sat. I went mute. It would have to wait until after school, our time together. When I got on the bus, I could barely breathe. I felt like the wind had been sucked out of me.

"I'm not going to make it here."

"What do you mean? Are you being overdramatic?"

"No, I'm serious," I said as quietly as possible. I needed her to see. "They hate me. They look at me like they wish I were dead."

"Fuck them," she said, "they're a bunch of snobby bitches. What can they do to you? You just need to get in their faces a little. Tell them your 'homegirls will be waitin' fo them lata.' Cough on them and tell them you have herpes. Freak them out a little."

She didn't get it. The hate on their faces would haunt my nightmares. She put her headphones on. For her, the problem was solved.

As the year passed, the snobby little queens iced her out as well; after all, she was no better than C'ville trailer trash in their eyes. But Tara had already started hanging out with a different crowd. She lingered in the halls with Jessie O, a platinum-blond Sun-In experiment who liked to kick the lockers with her white lace-up boots. Tara had begun to avert her eyes when she saw me coming, looking down as she hit the metal with the soft slap of her own fringed leather shoes. We didn't hang out after school for months.

One night, she invited me along for an evening of spreading egg yolks on suburban cars with her boyfriend. I went for the chance to see her, but I can't say that most of my eggs hit their targets; I've always been awkward when breaking the law. Afterward, we sat in the parking lot. I was as silent as John, who flirted with skinhead culture, and wrapped Tara into his bomber jacket. Looking past her, he gave me a cold stare that cut me to the quick. I left early for the night. Later, she would tell me they often had the same argument: "*Why* do you hang out with a wetback?"

"She's my best friend."

We still worked as busgirls two times a week at the Tex-Mex place where my mother waitressed; somehow, we still were close, even when we weren't. I felt more and more lost each day. By the end of the eighth grade, I'd earned a D average and missed about thirty-five days of school.

Oddly, despite my dismal report card, I turned to writing as a way to occupy time. A poem I'd submitted to a local contest had won an honorable mention. And eventually, I met other girls, kids I could talk comic books or TV with in the halls. But there weren't many I'd see outside of school. Except for those fleeting moments when Tara and I could be alone together again, nothing could touch the brutal honesty and increasing darkness of our after-school conversations.

"Do you think it's bullshit when people say they could live on nothing?" I asked one day when we were watching a show about punks in the seventies who'd run away from home. Her little brother, only a few years old, ran wildly through the room, as if to the beat of the Ramones soundtrack.

"Probably, but look at us. It's not like we had an easy ride." She looked around her dark living room, filled with broken toys and half-folded laundry. "It doesn't matter what you got. It's who you're with." I pictured John, his fist tight behind her back. I wasn't letting her get away with it.

"Who would you be with?" I asked, my voice cold. I scooted

an inch or two away on the couch. I wanted to make it hurt. "Could you leave him behind?" I pointed at her brother.

"I don't know," she said, as she pulled him close to her. "Probably not." We fell silent. On the TV, the punk girls were spray-painting anarchy symbols on their jackets. Their boyfriends were always close by, holding up the fabric and slipping it on their shoulders.

"How does it feel?" I asked. "When he puts his hands on you?"

"Honestly," she said. "It feels like shit. Because I know that no matter what, it will never be enough for me. I just can't get as close as I want. I know I shouldn't," she said, and looked up at me. "But I guess I can't help myself."

"Yeah," I said. "I know."

For a while, I didn't talk to her. I avoided her mother in supermarkets. I took extra shifts at work. A few weeks after our eighth-grade graduation, she invited me to a family party. Her stepdad made a special moonshine for us. He said it would put hair on our chests. "Y'all deserve it," he said, as he clapped us on our shoulders. "Hell, this is further than any of us ever got in school." We marked our rite of passage by mixing the bitter, clear concoction with wine coolers and Walmart soda.

Until we passed out cold.

In high school, the ground beneath us shifted. On the huge new territory, which fit a golf course and a full auditorium, there was room to reinvent ourselves. With more than a thousand students, hundreds of new microgroups had formed. Racist cheerleaders faded into the background among Asian American culture societies and Shakespeare appreciation groups. Tara and I had found new places to fit in. On the surface, we looked similar. Tara had dumped her boyfriend and skinhead crew, and we both wore the same generic nineties grunge attire: rock concert T-shirts, thick black mascara, colored tights, cutoffs, and thrift-store boots. We accidentally grabbed each other's flannel plaids at times because who could tell the difference? But underneath the surface, the chasm between us was growing. I joined the staff of the high school paper and volunteered at Amnesty International. My T-shirts started smelling more of Downy than patchouli or cigarette smoke.

My twilight hours were filling up with AP classes, study groups, and long hours at the school paper. After an intense talk with my older brother, who was now only a year away from starting college at the University of Chicago, I was beginning to understand: If I didn't start turning my grades around, I'd be living on the same dead-end block for the rest of my life. Tara also had gotten busier; she was shooting photos nonstop and organizing with PETA and had joined a theater group. We still saw each other on weekends and on the occasional afternoon. At parties, we drank vodka and orange juice as if nothing had changed; we covered for each other when our parents called.

One day our sophomore year, after we hadn't talked for a few weeks, she called me broken up, her voice thick with tears. "My mom fucked everything up," she said. "Tommy and Andrew are leaving. We have to move." The only father figure she'd ever known was taking her brother and going back to Arkansas.

Tara and her mom ended up moving to a small apartment near a shopping center in the middle of town. Once she learned how to drive, our junior year, she saved enough to buy a used Neon. It was a runner-up for the car she really wanted: the vehicle that would navigate our escape.

Later that year, I was watching her fold laundry after school when I heard her mother fumbling with the lock, her weight pushing the door more than the key. "Really, Mom?" I heard Tara say as she ran into the kitchen. "You can't even use the key right? You don't give a shit about this place. I can't wait to get the fuck out of here. You'll see. Michy and me are gonna drop out. We're going to Canada to look for my dad. And then what are you going to do? Break in?"

The story was that Tara's biological father had been forced to head back to Canada shortly after her conception to fulfill some military obligation. "Your father? I don't even know who that is, so you're gonna be lookin' a long time. I wouldn't bother heading all the way to Canada though, he could be anywhere." Her mother laughed hard as she fell into her chair. When Tara came back into the bedroom, her face was stone. She didn't cry, she didn't say a word. She just went right back to separating the underwear from the tank tops, and setting aside the pieces that would go into her suitcase, which was always ready, just in case.

"We could just drive," she said, looking me dead in the eye. "We'll just get on the road until we figure things out, like Thelma and Louise."

"Uh, you're gonna be doing a lot of driving . . ." I wasn't even close to getting my license.

"No, really." She grabbed my arm. "I don't care who drives . . .

you'll learn on the road anyway. We'll get a convertible. We'll go to the mountains on weekends and crash random parties. When we do go to school, we'll be the smartest girls in the room. We'll know how to live off the land."

"We could save our tip money," I said, getting excited. The pressure from the school paper, my family, and college prep exams was starting to get to me. I pictured us taking a break. We would make friends with college kids, and sleep on their couches. We would see redwood trees in Washington State.

"We'll figure it out; we can squat if we have to," she said.

"What, you mean like those anarchy chicks?" I said, remembering the punk girls who had slept on floors and been ready to party, their lips always painted bright at the rock clubs in London.

"Yeah, exactly," she said, her eyes wide now, her fingers tapping the side of her bed, the smell of ammonia from the darkroom wafting off her arms and filling the air. "Like those anarchy chicks . . . but who study, and don't belong to anyone."

From that point on, our escape was imminent. The idea was always there, infecting our dreams, even when we didn't talk.

When I started secretly hooking up with a friend who lived nearby, I waited before I told her. I had snuck him into my room after my mother left for work, and I wanted to savor the excitement of watching his black skin against my own in the afternoon light, feeling his hands in secret places for the first time. A few days later, I grabbed her in the cafeteria after lunch. It was time for an emergency meeting in the woods. But when I told her, I was the one in for a shock.

"Oh, I know," she said. "He told me. I hooked up with him the other day. It's so weird, right? It kind of just happened."

"Don't worry, though," she said, when she saw my face. "He likes you more. And besides, you'll forget about him later. When we're gone."

My anger and confusion didn't last long. Our brief fling fizzled on its own, and she was right, he wasn't going where I was headed, a place that I didn't yet know. But as the months passed, and I started going on college visits, everything started to come into focus. In the woods near our homes, during the summer of our junior year, we started to see the truth as we wandered through the thick silver of the trees and got lost, then found ourselves, time and time again.

"Do you really think we can do it?" she asked, looking intensely at the profile of my face. "Do you think we'll make it to college together? Be roommates?"

Instead of answering, I looked far, into the distance, where the trees finally tapered and faded into the road.

"You're not going with me, are you?" she said, closing her arms tight around her chest. "You already know where you're going."

"I'm sorry," I said, finally looking back at her. "I just can't."

"I know. I always did."

The last summer before I left for college, as we prepared to live away from each other for the first time in ten years, she would stop her car on the side of the road, always picking up the same conversation. "You'll never find anyone else like me," she said.

She lifted my hand and moved it between us. "You'll never find anything else like this. Do you know that?"

I didn't, at the time. I didn't know that other friends wouldn't tell you exactly what was on their minds, all the time. I didn't know that women didn't just naturally forgive everything of each other, that not everyone felt that no offense merited the silent treatment. That I would never feel another connection that I could depend upon so fully, one that needed no explanation. I can't even remember how many times I called her in a moment of stress, when my younger brother needed a ride to the hospital or my family was in the midst of a knock-down, drag-out fight. She was the only one who could step into a Spanish/English drama and not say a word. She would just get into her car and start driving.

I moved to a university eight hours away that fall. We both felt the sharp pang of distance quickly. She told me later she cried for hours after I left, listening to the same mixtapes we'd made together over and over again. On my new college campus, I looked for her in all the girls I met, determined to get wasted with any girl who cursed like a sailor or could pull a doughnut on an icy country road.

We saw each other when I came home, then later when she started school in nearby Carbondale, Illinois. If I got close to other friends in college, she would scrutinize us with slit eyes, looking for a connection we didn't have. She was surprised when I said I wanted to spend my junior year in Mexico.

"I thought you hated all of that," she said. "Those girls?

Your mother's family? *Spanish?* The food? What are you even going to do there?"

But how could she understand? It hadn't been as easy as I made it look to laugh off the jokes, the comments, and the invisibility I was still experiencing on my college campus. Mexican had to mean something different, more beautiful than the dirty streets by the bridge where my mother grew up or the taco-truck brown skin the girls in school saw when they looked at me. One day, in an art history class, I saw a series of photographs of the murals of David Alfaro Siqueiros. I studied the oversized, vivid faces and decided I had to see them in person. I wanted to be overwhelmed by the violence of color on that scale. I needed Zapatista-sympathizer friends, a Mexican professor lover, and the music of the Spanish language to teach me that I had somewhere to belong. A place I could be Mexican and American in my own way.

The beautiful thing about Tara was that, in the end, I didn't have to explain at all. When I didn't answer she just looked at me squinty and nodded her head. That space that she could no longer reach, the soft spot she'd poked under my ribs, was running on empty. And she would have to wait until I could find a way to fill myself up again. But I knew when I returned, she would still be standing there, at the edge of the woods, waiting. Our bond was sealed in blood.

A HEART-TO-HEART CONNECTION

Dr. Ana Nogales

For many years, I felt like an outsider. Growing up in Argentina, I experienced an unspoken separateness from kids my own age because my parents were immigrants, and Spanish was not their first language; Polish was. My mother and father had escaped from Europe before the Holocaust, but this was not something I could discuss with my friends. I was Jewish in a Catholic country, and my family's traditions were different than those of my playmates, with whom I desperately wanted to fit in.

My mother had a high regard for education and begged for my admission into a prestigious all-girls school in Buenos Aires. The student body was comprised primarily of children from the privileged class, and it was evident from my inability to join in their conversations about lavish vacations and stylish shopping trips that I was not in the same league as my classmates. I remember how ashamed I was about not being able to keep up with their fashions. Even though we were made to wear white smocks so that we would all look alike, my classmates would lift up their school uniforms to show what they were wearing underneath. I did not have a fashionable outfit to show off, so I chose to hide instead. Early on I learned how to be cautious around my classmates, as jealousy and rivalry were widespread. I stuck to my small group of friends, the ones who were also vulnerable to being teased about their outsider status. Together, we found safety from the snobs.

This feeling of not fitting in and not being entitled to full membership in the community would travel with me when I immigrated to the United States in 1979 at the age of twenty-eight. In fact, my sense of otherness intensified once I settled in California. Now I was a Spanish-speaking immigrant in an English-speaking world, cut off from non-Latinos and Latinos alike. In Los Angeles, the majority of Latinos are Mexican American, and at that point in my life I knew very little about their culture. And few Mexican Americans were familiar with the Argentinean way of life. When I began seeking employment as a psychologist, I did not understand what prospective employers meant when they told me that I was "overqualified" to work as a counselor. Then I realized that they perceived me as being unaware of the local culture. I wondered: *Were the immigrant experiences of those from other Latin American countries that different from my own?*

Yes they were.

I soon realized that I had to learn more than I had expected about the various Spanish-speaking immigrant cultures in Los Angeles. Even though we all spoke Spanish, we differed in our dialects, how we related to each other, and gender roles. It was not until much later that I discovered a more important truth: Despite our differences, we have so much in common. Slowly I began to understand that the experience of being Latina is very similar, not because we speak the same language, but because we love our families and friends, and we honor our values and customs with a similar passion. Over time, my connections to other Latinas continued to develop. I married a Mexican American man who became the father of my two youngest daughters, both beautiful mestizas. My oldest daughter was born in Argentina before I left for the U.S.

Even though my household was very Hispanicized, my attempts at forming closer bonds with other Latinos still proved difficult; I always had the feeling that there were those who believed that my desire to get close to the Chicano community was disingenuous.

I remember attending a business-related retreat in Washington, DC, in the early eighties, where the participants were all Mexican American. I decided I would finally express my feelings of isolation as a non–Mexican American Latina. I opened up and expressed myself, expecting that others would follow suit and sympathize. Well, that never happened. More than anything, I left the retreat convinced that I had made a fool of myself. The experience had made me feel so awkward that I began to distance myself emotionally, even more so than before. I told myself that it is inappropriate to combine business with personal disclosure. It wouldn't be until much later, when I learned the value of comadre gatherings, that I would discover how beautifully business can be merged with personal camaraderie—if the meeting is composed entirely of women.

After the business retreat, I became aware of how differently men and women comport themselves, and how women seem to act differently when in the company of men. I noticed that women are much more themselves when there are no men in the room. We can talk about business, but we can also ask others about their families and make comments about our colleague's stunning pair of shoes. Such alleged "small talk" is a no-no when men are involved, as it's considered unprofessional to become too personal.

Despite my initial reservations about putting myself out there, I continued to want to connect with other Latinas. Surprisingly, radio and television became my link to the Spanish-speaking community. I rarely got sick, but one day I took off from work and caught Enrique Gratas's show, *Mundo Latino*, on Univision, Los Angeles, and I had an epiphany. I told myself: "He is also Argentinean. I am going to call to tell him that I can come on his show and discuss psychology. I could talk about issues that concerned me and thousands of others—including the immigrant experience, loneliness, and the need to connect with each other." Little did I know that television would be my icebreaker for meeting other Latinas.

In addition to appearing on *Mundo Latino*, as a Spanish-speaking psychologist I was often asked to be a guest on television and radio shows that focused on psychological issues and relationship problems. Then, I was offered my own segment on a program called *Ella y El* on Univision. Dr. Juan Bustamante and I engaged in on-camera role-playing scenarios in order to highlight relationship dilemmas and offer our professional conflict resolution strategies. Those who called in to the show to share their problems and stories felt the emotional support not only from me and Dr. Bustamante, but from the thousands of viewers across southern California. We were there for each other in a meaningful way.

As I reached out to Latinos through the airwaves, they reached back, and I could feel a solid connection developing. I was offered my own daily radio show, *Aquí Entre Nos*, on La Voz, Southern California's first Spanish-language talk radio show. Most of the callers were Latinas who spoke of problems with their families, in their relationships, and at work. Not only were they suffering from the particular circumstances they described, but also from the isolation and despair of not being able to share their problems with a trusted friend. In the callers' voices I heard an intense longing. These were women who needed to talk, who needed to connect with others who would understand them. They were Latinas living in a society that often caused us to disconnect from each other. And there were others who never had the courage to call in to the show, but who told me years later how much they learned from listening to the voices of other women.

It became obvious to me that when we become disconnected from one another, we are more prone to anxiety, depression, and hopelessness. But when we reach out to other women, we become empowered. I began to witness the little miracles that can happen when Latinas talk and listen to each other straight from the heart. A stranger, who tells her story of having been abandoned by the father of her children, or abused by her husband, connects with another stranger listening at home who has endured the same experiences. Such an authentic exchange can create a meaningful bond. Suddenly, strangers are linked, connected by their need and their offering of mutual support. These talk shows were my first introduction to the idea of comadreship and all its benefits.

My daily television show continued to bring women together for the purpose of airing their troubles and getting in touch with other women who had "been there." There was a thirst not only for a psychologist's professional advice but for the kind of on-air peer counseling that was proving to be a lifeline to so many

Latinas. After the *Los Angeles Times* did a story featuring my show, one thing led to another. A literary agent asked if I would be interested in writing a book for Latino couples that would serve as a guide to solving relationship and parenting issues. Of course, I said yes. During the book tour, women came up to me relating their experiences and expressing how they had benefited from hearing other women describe what they, too, had been through.

Meanwhile, Latinas whom I serve in both my private practice and through the nonprofit psychological service organizations that I founded echoed this sentiment. By the same token, when we can share our successes and insight, we can become inspirational to others. That is how my book *Latina Power!* was born. I believe that Latinas embody profound strengths and that we can empower each other to develop them. All too often, we fail to give ourselves the credit we deserve because of our family backgrounds, psychological issues, or cultural biases.

My comadre awareness had certainly been raised and I deeply appreciated the many women whom I had the privilege to interview and connect with. But it wasn't until I met Dr. Nora de Hoyos Comstock that the message behind las comadres resonated to its fullest. During an interview with the *Washington Post,* I was asked about the meaning of comadres. I answered by discussing the ways in which women can benefit from the focused attention, support, and friendship of a caring comadre. Afterward, the reporter asked me if I was aware of a group called Las Comadres Para Las Americas; I wasn't, but I soon found out that there was an extraordinary woman behind this organization.

Nora believed in the power of comadres, and she founded the organization based on her own need to be around other Latinas. Of course, she intuited that this need of hers was not unique. Well aware of all that we have to give each other, Nora unleashed her plan to bring us together. I discovered that Nora lives her life commanded by her heart. Unlike those who focus solely on themselves, Nora knows that the answer to prosperity and abundance is to build a strong community. And that is exactly what she dedicates her life to. She stays focused so that the rest of us can also perceive her vision and experience it as clearly as she does. Unafraid to commit to a life fueled by her passionate energy, she simply goes for it. When her heart tells her something is well worth the time, energy, sweat, and money, she commits to it and sees it to fruition. And that is what I love about her.

I connected with Nora immediately. Getting to know her, I could finally let go of those lingering feelings of alienation and otherness that I had lived with all my life. I knew I had found a kindred soul. And through her spirit I was able to assert mine. I asked Nora how I could begin re-creating in California what she had done in Texas, and soon after, we had our own comadrazos in Southern California —which would later expand to other areas on the West Coast and beyond. Word was spreading that when we participate in a comadrazo we are free to talk about ourselves, ask for what we need, strategize, or share our frustrations, aspirations, and ambitions. We feel our power when we gather together.

As a fellow comadre, Yolanda Hernandez, put it: "Las Co-madres has been my pillar of strength in my most depressing moments, my window of opportunity to amazing connections, and my lifeline to lifelong friendships. For the past seven years I have been carried, nurtured, energized, inspired, cleansed; and I have cried, laughed, hugged, sung, danced, shopped, and prayed with my group of Las Comadres. Without the companionship and strength of this group, I could not have survived my bout with cancer, the loss of my mother to lung cancer, the loss of my brother to alcohol and AIDS. I would not have been inspired to go back to school. I would not have met so many amazing Lati-nas who have left me in awe of their talents and wisdom. Most of all, I have never felt alone or felt so empowered as I feel today."

Yolanda's experience is not unique. Many Latinas find simi-lar inspiration in the comadre groups that began with Nora's vision. Because of these profound feelings we experience when we get together, I am compelled to create innovative programs and offer resources that can help more women. But the process of seeing each project through to completion is not always easy. Sometimes I take on more than is womanly possible, or I feel frustrated that I cannot tackle five crises at once. Whenever I question my ability to see my plans successfully through to the end, all I have to do is call forth my image of Nora and Las Comadres. I see their faces, feel their smiles and their support, and I keep going. It doesn't matter that I cannot see them face to face, because Las Comadres are always with me in spirit.

Walking into that first gathering, I felt like I was home. What I found most satisfying about becoming a comadre with so many wonderful women was that we could generously give of ourselves with no sense of rivalry or *chisme,* but rather, a spirit of camaraderie and love. There is a sense of sisterhood based in the horizontal style of this organization, with no need to compete for elections or power roles, since these do not exist.

There was a sense of familiarity, even though I had never before met any of the women with whom I was exchanging stories and experiences. We were there to build our community, and we felt exhilarated to be part of this new comadre organization, a heart-to-heart adventure. We learned that we each had felt "different" in one way or another, that at some point in our lives we had felt we did not belong, that we were marginalized from society, sometimes confused about what our role was within our communities.

There is no doubt that women and men react differently when they need emotional support. Most of the time, women are not asking for direction or instructions. Women want to be listened to, and when we are heard, we can arrive at our own conclusions. By connecting with each other, we have authentic friendship on our side—an essential in the life of every woman. All human beings are social animals; we all need our friends for social support. As Latinas, this is especially true. It is often said that we do not choose our family, but that we do choose our friends. When Latinas say *mi casa es tu casa,* we really mean it.

In fact, a study by UCLA researchers confirmed what many of us had always suspected: Comadres are beneficial to your health. Another study showed that people who had no friends increased their risk of death over a six-month period. In another, those who had the most friends over a nine-year period cut their risk of death by more than 60 percent.

Moreover, research conducted by Dr. Joseph Flaherty of the University of Illinois–Chicago found that "strong social support networks help prevent depression in women, but didn't have a significant effect in men." Therefore, women need to nurture friendships even more than men do. Not only is it our natural tendency to seek out friends when we are in crisis, but it is also physiologically advantageous.

When women are surrounded by supportive women, they become more hopeful. When we join with other women and learn that our experiences are similar to those of our comadres, we create a sacred space in which to heal. The women in our group therapy sessions recovering from an abusive relationship or sexual assault have discussed what a difference it makes when they see that they are not alone. And when women in abusive relationships gather together in a support group, they usually find a way out of those relationships more easily.

As I continued to connect with comadres all over the United States, Nora's vision continued to expand. She dreamed of taking Las Comadres Para Las Americas internationally and the next thing we knew, a group of eight comadres that included Nora and me were meeting at Lucy Muñoz's home in London. Many of the Latinas we met were residing there temporarily on work permits or for other business purposes. Others were there because their husbands or partners asked them to be there for them. Their sense of estrangement was intense, and coming together at an intimate comadrazo was like finding their long-lost sisters.

Wherever comadres meet they express the same sense of joy

that I felt the first time I attended a comadrazo, and which I continue to feel at every one I attend. Surrounded by supportive women, our lives are made easier and sweeter. As Latinas we are lucky, we don't just have friends, we have comadres—women with whom we can enjoy a mutually nurturing relationship, who we consider spiritual or honorary family members. When we become comadres we each take on the role of a caring woman who helps to nurture and develop the other's dreams and projects. Comadres also take on the roles of sister, ally, *tía*, counselor, cousin, mentor, advocate, confidante, and more.

The future of our community depends on the wisdom of our women. We are not only in charge of our families, we are responsible for the wellness of future generations. We share the responsibility for our children and their education, for our communities, and for providing better opportunities for us all. There is no need for any of us to feel like outsiders. Everywhere I travel I find comadres, and there is always someone who just learned about us and wants to join, someone who wants to cure that alienating sense of isolation.

We have the power to influence social change. As we continue to support our comadres, more Latinas are seeking higher education, opening their own businesses, engaging in scientific research, excelling in academia and the arts, holding political office—and shaping a future that reflects our wisdom, passion, and values. We still have a long way to go, but our hearts are in it. And as comadres we are making it happen. Together.

COMPADRES

Luis Alberto Urrea

L ove is the color when hopelessness catches fire.

My comadre lives on a hilltop in Tijuana that used to house the Tijuana municipal garbage dump. The *pepenadores*, as they call them in Mexico, took over the dump in a kind of Occupy Basura movement and squatted there. They're called *paracaidistas* in Mexico—paratroopers. And the law states that if a community of squatters settles and maintains the neighborhood long enough, they have some leeway in the legal wrangling over the land that is sure to erupt. If they manage to coerce the municipality to provide any services at all—water, electricity—then the neighborhood is usually recognized by the government. In this case, they took the roughest parts of the *dompe*, where the poorest garbage pickers made their camps, and built little houses and ran garden hoses down from the hilltop water tank to pirate *agua*; then they got Tijuana to install some electric lights so their young women could come home on the *burra* buses at night in safety.

Voilà: A new barrio rose, quite literally, from the ashes.

It has in no way been a fun place to live, although it is home. Everybody knows everybody else. There are good parties there—after all, it's the old dompe. If you want a party, you throw it, and if you want light, you set fire to some wood in the middle of your street. As my comadre says, "In the United States, they don't know how to party. You can't light bonfires in the street in San Diego. *Mejor me quedo aquí en mi tierra.*"

*   *   *

There have been long seasons of gang warfare between the barrio and the one below it. Knifings and stabbings, then came the shootings. There have been health issues—you can imagine living in a house made of old wooden pallets built on thirty years of festering trash. When it rains, as I have described in previous books, the ground sometimes erupts in little geysers of methane gas. People sometimes sink garbage mines in the land to see what fossils of treasure lie beneath. Canned food can be found in these narrow pits. Toys, plates, coats. Miscarriages, cancer, blindness—all the toxic byproducts of sneaky industrial dumping—seep through the populace. Once, the city's abortion clinics unloaded human tissue on the ground not far from my comadre's shack. And imagine the people at the bottom of the hill, for Tijuana has sprawled into canyons nobody would have lived in twenty years ago, and the water that filters down out of the dompe, and feeds the brown little creeks in the bottomland, is a chemist's nightmare.

Then there are the drugs. Drugs started out to be the usual poverty highs: glue sniffing, the occasional marijuana. But now, in the era of the narcos, things are more dangerous. More complicated.

A mile from my comadre's house, one of the big marijuana storehouses sits, still punctured like a colander by machine-gun fire after the Mexican army slaughtered the narcos inside. And about a quarter mile from this haunted building is the bridge where narcos were hanging nude, tortured human bodies on ropes. Men took one of my comadre's daughters hostage for a week, and nobody talks about what happened to her in their house. I was far away and could not help them. The problem with having extended family in such situations—as many Latino families know all too well—is that we here in Disneyland only hear about the terrible stories after they happen.

My comadre is a badass: She can take you out with her bare hands. She once beat up a *morra* when she was nine months pregnant. She killed a pit bull with a wrench after it bit my goddaughter. She has homemade tattoos on her arms. We love each other very much.

And I am always happy when I'm in her barrio, even though sometimes mysterious men in SUVs come along and demand to know my name.

Let us call the barrio Fraccionamiento Juan Rulfo. It would be unwise to direct attention to the actual place, given the current climate on the underside of the border. You couldn't get any farther from where I live, the *Leave It to Beaver* green suburbs west of Chicago. I think, however, that even though our lives are from different solar systems, one could make an interesting correlation between trash pickers and writers. After all, we both spend our days sifting through the detritus to find odd little gems from which we can make something useful.

We can safely speak her nickname, I think—even though there was some evidence that the Juárez women-killings might be spreading to Juan Rulfo. She was worried because men had tried to grab one of her other daughters and drag her into a truck, and neighbors found a murdered schoolgirl behind the

secondary school about halfway downhill between her and the
dope warehouse. In relationships, it pays to weigh your words.
Now, in writing about my beloved border, it can be a mortal
choice.

So I will tell you the name I always knew her by, though she
no longer uses it. She grew up. And there are many women with
the same name. And she has appeared in my border books under
it. It's the way I still think of her: Negra.

You can read about her in my first books: *Across the Wire*
and *By the Lake of Sleeping Children*. She has been on TV, she
has been on radio, she has graced newspaper pages, she has appeared in picture books (Jack Lueders-Booth's bracing *Inherit
the Land*). She has even appeared on NPR, in a memorable epi-
sode of *This American Life*. All because of some obscure words I
scribbled in generally unknown books. Truly, we labor beneath
different suns, Negra and I. She was baffled and outraged that
she once earned six hundred dollars for addressing a convention
of border journalists in a Tijuana hotel. "Wait," she said. "You
get paid money for *talking*?"

I won't overburden you with the old tales of how we met,
aside from a quick sketch. But I'd like to address the situation
of the friendship between us. Of the strong bond that is often
stretched and even torn, but never by us. Events and the roiling
of history separate us, sometimes for years.

But the bond holds.

It is possible for men and women to be deep friends, I think.
It is necessary. I want to throw a rock through my TV every
time a successful female character in a popular show has to
sleep with her handsome A) attending doctor, B) law firm se-

nior partner, C) pool boy, D) David Duchovny. I was raised by women, and women have always been my best pals. Wife included. What might be harder than true friendship, I think, is to be compadres across the terrible gap of poverty and hopelessness. Negra's hunger convicts us at every meal.

I take comfort in an old line of Bono's: "I can't change the world, but I can change the world in me."

I have helped my comadre over the years, but she is the one who has blessed me.

Short version: I worked in a crew of what my publishers' bio notes call "relief workers." Pseudomissionaries, let's face it. A Christian organization that took food, clothing, medicine, water, portable shower stalls, toys, shampoos, doughnuts, hope, playtime, and, yes, preaching to the poor in Tijuana. I had been at loose ends after college, and though this work was not as cool as, say, being an extra in a Chuck Norris movie (yeah, I'm BAD), it was overwhelming and meaningful and transformative. One of the places we worked was the Tijuana dompe. Students who sit through my frequent university visiting lectures can tell you I am quite proud of being the only author on any bill who got his start in the Tijuana dumps.

Negra was a small girl when I met her. She was six. I was in my early twenties. She taught me how to pick trash—it is a real skill. You'd have to apprentice yourself to a pro to get the hang of it. Just the mastery of the long pole you use to sift garbage and whack angry rats is a kind of samurai talent you have to learn. I was poor, and I was self-pitying about it; Negra's life caught me up short, however. I suddenly saw what "poor" meant—it wasn't me. I had shoes.

Extremely dire circumstances caused her, at twelve, to become the common-law wife of my compadre, Jaime. This happened during one of our extended separations. You see, I had gone from the dompe to go teach Expository Writing at Harvard. How'd that happen? I'm still not sure. When I left, she was a kid who had to see a map drawn in the dirt to understand where I was going. She wore black rubber *chola*-bracelets, and she placed one on my wrist so the Harvard *rucas* would know who I belonged to. I wore it till it rotted off.

I came home years later and found her. It wasn't easy. She didn't have writing skills, and she didn't have a street address even if I were to send a letter. A telephone was out of the question. So finding her was somewhat of a miracle, not unlike the whole Harvard thing. She and Jaime were living in a chicken coop. She was pregnant. She had tried to commit suicide. "I took a bottle of sleeping pills," she told me. "All that happened was I got a really good sleep."

Is it bad that we laughed till we cried when she told me this?

We managed to cobble together funds for her to have her baby in a clinic downtown. Thank God for rich-kid friends with fat inheritance money and Amnesty International urges. That baby became my godchild. La Honis, as close to "Honey" as they could get.

I kicked into high rescue gear: I was going to be Jaime and Negra's compadre! And I was not going to see this family live out the winter in a drafty chicken coop with scorpions and tarantulas and black widows everywhere! No way, compa. So I enlisted a biker pal who somehow wrangled a huge flatbed truck from some church, and we collected old garage doors from a garage-door replacement company in San Diego, then went head-to-head with recalcitrant and angry Mexican border cops seeking a juicy *mordida* from us for smuggling in so much lumber. It was like a Mickey Rooney movie—in Spanish. *Orale, kids!* Let's build a *casa!*

The neighbors all bore the heavy doors on their shoulders. We brought in two loads. It was a barrio phenomenon. I could have printed business cards that read, OCCUPATION: HERO. Jaime and his homeboys got out hammers and screwdrivers and saws and salvaged tarpaper and a couple of possibly stolen windows, and set to it with boisterous heave-ho's and loud, cursing laughter. Damn, it was beautiful.

My mother had died, which is why I had returned from Boston. I smuggled her refrigerator to them—their first refrigerator, ever. I took them her television. And I took Negra her set of art books because Negra loved beautiful things, even in the dump. Suddenly, we could drink cold sodas and look through Monet, Cézanne, Van Gogh, Seurat books. Imagine that scene, in a garage-door house in the middle of a garbage dump looking at Impressionists while sipping Mexican Coca-Cola out of plastic glasses dug out of the garbage. Perhaps the only artist capable of catching the full strangeness of this scene would have been Salvador Dalí.

And suddenly, it was time for the baptism.

In the days before we baptized La Honis, Negra took me on a tour of the cardinal points of her journey. Here was the shack where her baby brother had burned to death in his crib. Here was the spot where Jaime had built her a hut. Here was the corner where she took out the *morra* with the big mouth and showed her what an ass-kicking by a pregnant woman felt like. Across town in the new dump, she showed me a terrible spot. A spot that was so stunning, that I didn't even feel revulsion or horror. I stood there, fingering the remains and thought, *how odd and interesting*.

Her uncle had lived in a shack made of aluminum siding on the edge of a dirt cliff that would soon be buried under the rising mountain of garbage at the new site. If I had been more prescient then, I would have known that the favorite bugaboo of my conservative friends—IMMIGRATION (key in horror-movie orchestration)—was already on its way to being overshadowed and annihilated by narco war. The signs were already on the ground, even then. And Negra's uncle had somehow been fingered as a player of some sort in the dompe dope game: Bad men came after him to steal the cocaine they thought he had in his aluminum hut. He barricaded himself within and refused to allow them to enter. So they piled brush all around the hut and poured gasoline over it and lit it. They baked him to death.

There is no way to tell you this gently, or prettily. It isn't pretty. But it is deeply in the core of my comadre's struggle. "They melted him," she said. "There was grease and bones here." Perhaps you can understand my inability to process this information. My tiny comadre, my Negra, holding my hand while her girls played around us, saying her uncle had been *rendered while alive*. She said it in a tone of voice one might use to say, "It's raining today."

But to make her point, she reached into the brick-lined pit where his little wood-burning oven used to be. She dragged out a piece of green carpet—old bathroom carpet. It was heavy with coagulated grease. It looked like spilled cooking lard.

"This is my uncle," she said.

I recently spoke at the University of Illinois in Champaign. They had somehow coerced three hundred freshmen into reading one of my novels that features the dompe in one section. Over dinner, I asked the students what they wanted to talk about. One young woman said, "Just don't depress us anymore talking about dead people."

Fortunately, grace falls on us all. Even when we don't recognize it. Even in the dompe.

The day of the baptism was sunny and gentle. The dompe church had been built by the locals out of scrap wood. They had built rough pews. They didn't have a priest, but a circuit-riding young Father who made the heroic rounds of Tijuana and environs, and they timed their masses and sacred events to his schedule. He pulled in and was informed that there was a baptism, and he fetched his fancy robes and I handed him some folding green, and the people rang the church bell. Well, not really. There was no church bell. But they had hung a car axle off a chain outside the church, and one of Jaime's homeboys whacked it good and hard with a crowbar.

There it was. Smoky, dirty. Smelly. Hardworking good people from whom most of their media attackers would flee from in terror. Bloody, raw knuckles. Even lice. People smelling like sweat and sickness and bad years. Everyone in that room illuminated with joy. Everyone there as filthy and disrespected and forgotten and cursed. As if Jesus himself were about to walk into a gathering in Canaan. Everyone there holy.

La Honis, however, seemed to channel the devil when she realized this weird gringo guy in white robes was about to pour water over her head.

I left again. I had a life to lead, I had books to write, I had my own mistakes and bad mojo to confront. But this time I left her with her first bank account. The bankers didn't want her to enter when we went downtown—she wore her best shiny gold lamé slippers. They stopped us at the door, this odd couple: the tiny Indian woman (Tarascan) and the big Irish-looking Spanish-speaking dude holding a baby. What must they have thought?

The bank manager, a nasty little bastard in a tight suit and bleached hair, stopped us and said Negra could not enter. I could. But, really, what were we thinking bringing her type to the bank? I fanned out $1,200 in American twenties and said, "This is hers. Can she come in now?"

Oh, the bowing; oh, the manners.

I also had Western Union, that mainstay of the remittance money tide that flooded Mexico. "La Western," they called it. Negra would call me collect from a pay phone near the little bodega in Juan Rulfo and tell me how much she needed.

When I returned, I returned because National Public Radio wanted me to find her. A producer followed me around with a mic and a recorder. It was, again, surreal. And this was the era when Negra made her impossible six hundred dollars for talking.

We were put up in the ritzy Camino Real. By any measure, a

fancy hotel. Negra was too scared of the rich people to go alone, so she took her eldest daughter, Nayeli. They put on their best clothes, and we arrived at the hotel, and they balked at the escalator. They had not ridden escalators.

As we rose, and the great marble walls and the overhead lights revealed themselves, Negra turned to me and said, "I don't belong here, compadre."

"Why not?"

"We are poor."

I said, "The only difference between you and these *cabrones* is that they have money."

We entered the vast lobby, and there, to Negra and Nayeli's shock, sat several Mexican telenovela actors. One guy with silver hair was reading a magazine, and they gasped, "Es Don ____!"

"Go say hello," I suggested.

"We can't!"

"Go on. He'll love it."

"Ay, Luis!"

It was an agony of self-doubt, but they went. And he turned on his billion-watt white smile at them as if they were fine ladies from Hollywood. He signed autographs for them.

The young woman at the desk, trained to have exquisite manners, called them "Ma'am" and "Miss." We rose to their room, and I wondered what they'd make of it. The Camino Real filtered the entire hotel's water system so tourists could drink and bathe safely. We entered their room and two things happened immediately: Negra went to the beds and felt the mattresses while Nayeli went right to the bathroom and turned on the water in the bathtub to see it spill out. The next thing that happened was Nayeli falling on the bed and asking, "Luis, how do we get MTV?"

They were hungry. I showed them the room service menu. It had pictures of the food.

"But we have no money."

"Your hosts will pay."

Nayeli found pizzas. She called them "piksas." I showed her the number to call and went next door to my room. A few minutes later, my phone rang—it was Nayeli.

"What number do I dial to order ice cream?" she asked.

It only took one night of being called "Ma'am," of ordering room service, and soaking in long, hot bubble baths while MTV blasted the room, for my comadre to completely transform. The dompe? Never happened. Being humble, scared? Not for her. She awoke haughty. She awoke large and in charge.

We went down to the restaurant and she sent back three different plates of food.

"Badly cooked," she informed the waitress.

After breakfast, she didn't want me to leave a tip.

"This place," she announced, waving a grand dame's hand around, "doesn't impress me."

You cannot save your friends or loved ones by throwing money at them. You simply can't. You have to find a way to make their dreams come true. In Negra's case, it was always about independence, and the safety of her girls. She parted ways with Jaime in a telenovela kind of way—bad girlfriends, that kind of thing. And she was picking trash again, against her will. She was working La Western pretty hard, too, I will admit. I had to learn that when the inevitable catastrophes happened, it was not my job to control what they chose to do with the money. When, for example, it was extremely urgent for them to get bus tickets to Michoacán to attend the funeral of an aunt, I sent the three hundred dollars right away. We could not afford it at the time, my wife and I, but we could afford it more than my comadre. When, later, she admitted they hadn't gone to Michoacán but had bought a really fancy dress so Nayeli could go to a dance . . . well. I realized that money was magic to them—it didn't really make sense. And, really, why not a dress? I had always wanted them to enjoy beauty, not just survival.

It was Negra who provided the solution. It taught me to trust. Trust the process of life and friendship. Negra realized that she had a dream. This was a major development, because we had experienced a deeply uncomfortable moment together based on this term, "dream."

I had naively, in my young author way, asked her once, "What is your big dream?"

"*¿Qué?*"

"Your dream. What do you dream about?"

"*No comprendo.*"

"Your dream. Your dream. For the future."

"What dream?"

"Negra! What do you dream about. For tomorrow? What is your hope for the future."

She looked at me helplessly and said, "I honestly don't understand what you are talking about."

But perhaps that awkward moment laid a seed. You never know. One day she called me collect and told me she had a dream for the future now. I asked what it was.

"Beauty parlor."

I sputtered.

"I want to be a hairdresser to the dump ladies. Everybody wants to be pretty, compadre!"

And she wanted to sell makeup, too. She wanted to be the dompe Avon lady selling brown "leepee-steekee" to the ladies. My response was something like: "I, I, I, I . . ."

But she had done research. She had made a list of what she wanted. Shades of mascara and lipstick, weird haircutting machines, combs, spritzers, and money to rent a shed. I had never heard anything like this plan in my life. Even in my novels, a scenario like the beauty operator of the garbage dump would have been impossible. Wasn't it Mark Twain who said something like: Fiction has to make sense, even if life doesn't?

Suddenly, it was not a handout, but an investment. Negra did not like asking for help. She did like asking for help to do something about her lot in life. We bought the stuff. She rented half of a guy's shack and set up a chair, and she cut hair and did perms and sold leepee-steekee.

Amen.

I once asked my comadre why our girls had never picked trash like she had. *Oh no. No no.* She shook her head.

"My girls," she said, "will never experience what I did."

"Tell me why."

"I was at the dompe one day, working. The girls were off to the side, waiting in the shade. You know how, when you're busy—really, really busy—you can't stop for anything? The work's going well, you're hustling, you can't take a break."

I nodded.

"It was like that. And when those days happen, even if you have a rock in your shoe, you can't stop right away to shake it out."

"Right."

"I had a rock or a stick in my shoe. But I couldn't stop. All morning. So when a break finally came, I sat down and took off my shoe to shake out the rock. And do you know what it was?"

"No."

"It was a human finger."

There was nothing to say to that. Nothing.

"I vowed on that day that my daughters would never in their lives enter the garbage and work the way I did."

We are apart again. Life has intruded, as it will always do. But they have prepaid cell phones in Tijuana now. Mi comadre calls me, sometimes while I'm on book tour. "¿Onde andas ahora, compadre?" she'll ask. It always makes her laugh when I'm in some place she's never heard of. "Seattle? ¡Ay, compadre!"

I think of her every day, even when I cannot see her.

And I know she'll feel me writing this story.

She'll be calling in a minute.

ACKNOWLEDGMENTS

Comadres, how can I thank you for all your passion and support? Thank you for preserving and celebrating our culture and for being there for each other. I cannot acknowledge you all by name, but know that each one of you is in my heart. This anthology owes a debt of gratitude to the comadres who worked diligently to make it happen: our editor Johanna Castillo; Esmeralda Santiago, our initial book club spokesperson; Adriana V. López, our anthology editor; and Adriana Domínguez Ferrari, whose behind-the-scenes work made all the difference. A special thank-you to Amy Tannenbaum and the rest of the Atria team for their work on this book, as well as the anthology's authors, because as busy as they were, they made time to do this for us.

My dear comadre Laura López Cano, whom I commissioned to create Las Comadres' beautiful logo, *muchas gracias*. Laura and I worked with comadre Sally Velázquez to Photoshop the original image, and Sally's generosity and time are much appreciated. Mary Armesto also played a part in the transition from the original image to the reinvented one that graces our web pages, bookmarks, posters, and all that we put our minds to.

The Board of Directors of Las Comadres has been very supportive during the twelve years of our existence: Annabelle Arteaga, PhD, Elizabeth Garcia, JD, Ana Nogales, PhD, Veronica Rivera, JD, Gloria Williams, and Irene Williams. Past board members include Bibi Lobo, Nimia Ramos Beauchamp, JD, and Deanna Rodriguez. *Mil gracias* to every one of you.

The Las Comadres organization could not exist without the coordinators who keep the city networks going. There would be no real organization without: Lourdes Abadín, Dora María Abreu, Cristina Abreu, Ofelia Allen, Aurora Anaya-Cerda, Ana Arelys Cruz, Amanda Arizola, Annabelle Arteaga, PhD, María Avelino, Cristina Ballí, Natasha Bannan, Sunny Bañuelos, Melinda Barrera, Roció Benedicto, PhD, Sylvia Benítez, Debbie Bonilla, Margie Brickey, Patricia Briotta, Gabriela Bucio, Ada Gabriela Bueno Pulliam, María Cardes, Catherine Cardoso, Gloria Casas, Camila Ceballos, Rosa Celis-Rodriguez, Loretta Charles, Denise Chavez, Janis Chavez, Frances Colon, Alejandra Cossio, Rose Costas, Lori Crouch, Carmen Cruz, Silvia Cruzo, Nora Díaz, Sylvia E. Camacho, Nori Cuellar Mora, PhD, Amelia de Jesús, Lilli de Cair, Linda de la Cruz, Rosalba Domínguez, Stephanie Elizondo Griest, Clara Engel, Yolanda Escandón, Fern Espino, PhD, Jocelyn Feliciano, Charley Ferrer, PhD, María Ferrer, Amira Flores, Ariana Flores, Stella Flores, PhD, Christy García Martínez, Dalia García, Edna García, Vicky García, Bobbie Garza-Hernández, Susan Garretson, San Juanita Godufsky, Vickie Gómez, Adriana González,

Christine González, Verónica Guerra, Yolanda Guzmán, Yolanda Hernández, Linda Hernández, Ana Hershberger, Alicia Higgins, Marcela Hincapié, Ángela Hope, Karla Jaramillo, Helen Jiménez Ulloa, Adriana Jiménez, Nancy Johnson, Margie Kensit, Demetra Koelling, Isabel Lemus, Diana León, Bibi Lobo, Adriana López, Connie López, Diana López Axthelm, Cynthia López, Raquel Lynch, Lori Maes, Lolita Mancheno-Smoak, Ángela Martin, Araceli Martínez-Rose, Érica Martínez Rose, Raquel Martínez, Sylvia G. Martínez, Yvette Mayo, Martha Medina, Jacqueline Méndez, María Angélica Mendoza, Bernice Miera, Beatriz Mieses, Nuria Miller, Clotilde Molina, Elizabeth Moncevais, Carmen Montañés, María Montenegro, Ana Morales, Ana Nogales, PhD, Ydalmi Noriega, Ginz Núñez, PhD, Virginia Ornelas, Ángeles Ortega, Jasmine Jina Ortíz, Clara Ospina, Melinda Palacio, Addy Pérez Mau, Maribel Pérez Tur, Sandra Pérez, Ofelia Philo, Michele Ping, Carmen Quiles, Shelly Quintana, Elena Ramos, Nimia Ramos Beauchamp, Evelyn Reyes, Marielis Rivera, Francis Robles, Imelda Rocha, Sandra Rodríguez Barrón, María Rojo, Laura Rolandelli, Ana Cecilia Rosado, Leyden Rovelo, Sally Ruiz, Lupita Sáenz Eckoff, Ruth Saenz, Jayni Saenz, Rachael Saldivar, Jennifer Sánchez, Terry Saucedo, Dyannette Siaca, Patricia Sosa, Christine Soto, Rebeca Summers, Ana Sweeney, Michelle Talan, Lourdes Tinajero, Lisa Torres Stonebeck, Dora Tovar, Gloria Uribe, Josie Valdez, Laura Valdez Karam, Ángela Valdivia, BB Vásquez, Palmira Vásquez Ginsberg, Kathy Vega, Melody Vela, Diana Velásquez, Myrna Vélez, Gloria Williams, and Alejandra Zavala.

We are so fortunate to have our book club. Thank you to

the Association of American Publishers, especially Tina Jordan, Marlene Scheuermann, and Becca Worthington, the publishers who share their books, and our book club coordinators and discussion leaders who are devoted to reading and sharing our authors. Thank you for making this dream a reality and for keeping it going: Blanca Alvarado, PhD, María Betancourt, Luz Betancourt, Nohelia Canales, Catalina Cantú, Teresa Carbajal Ravet, Leslie Colon-Lebron, Erika Córdova, Lori Crouch, Yolanda Cuesta, Martha Curcio, Karin Dávalos, Laura De Anda, Lilli De Cair, Nora Díaz, María Ferrer, Adriana Frías, Cristina Glez Novoa, Gabriela González, Sylvia Hernández Kauffman, Demetra Koelling, Mary López, Liana López, Araceli Martínez-Rose, Linda Mazón Gutiérrez, Sylvia Mendoza, Edith Mercer, Carmenza Millan, Ydalmi Noriega, Anna Núñez, Nicole Ortiz, Pam Portillo, Cynthia Ramos, Nimia Ramos Beauchamp, Gayle Rana, Leyden Revelo, Lara Ríos, Frances Robles, Lois Rodríguez, Vanessa Rodríguez, Lissette Rodríguez, Silvia Sofía San Miguel, Jennifer Sánchez, María Solís, Rachael Torres, Nissheneyra Urizandi, Delila Vásquez, Ada Vilageliu Díaz, Stefanie Von Borstel, Anne Warman, Martha Weeks, Gloria Williams, and Alma Willard.

Jack Bell, how can I thank you? For twelve years you have labored alongside me and kept Las Comadres going and growing. The late nights, the long hours, and the financial support. I don't know how you have stayed married to me, but bless you.

Con cariño,

Nora

CONTRIBUTORS

NORA DE HOYOS COMSTOCK, PhD, is the national and international founder of Las Comadres Para Las Americas and has served as the organization's president and CEO since its founding. She received her PhD from the University of Texas at Austin in educational administration and was a fellow at the National Hispana Leadership Institute in Washington, DC. In 2006, Dr. Comstock received a lifetime achievement award for her service to the community from the Hispanic Professional Women's Association, and in 2007 was named one of the Top 25 Hispanic Influencers in Austin, Texas. She was given Maybelline's Beauty of Education Award and was honored as one of the 25 Mujeres del Año 2011 by *Sucesos: El Periódico de la Comunidad Hispana* in Houston, Texas. Las Comadres Para Las Americas was the recipient of a 2011 Community Leadership Award by the University of Texas at Austin for the organization's commitment and dedication to promoting social justice, increasing opportunities for inclusion, and improving access to education.

CAROLINA DE ROBERTIS is the author of the novels *Perla* and *The Invisible Mountain,* which was an international bestseller translated into fifteen languages, a *San Francisco Chronicle* Best Book of the Year, an *O, The Oprah Magazine* 2009 Terrific Read, and the recipient of Italy's Rhegium Julii Prize. She is also the translator of various works of Latin American literature, most recently *The Neruda Case* by Roberto Ampuero. De Robertis is the recipient of a 2012 Fellowship from the National Endowment for the Arts. She lives in Oakland, California, with her wife and son. Visit her at www.carolinaderobertis.com.

REYNA GRANDE entered the United States from Mexico as an undocumented immigrant at the age of ten to be reunited with her father. She went on to become the first in her family to obtain a higher education. She holds a BA and an MFA in creative writing. Her debut novel, *Across a Hundred Mountains,* received a 2006 El Premio Aztlan Literary Award, a 2007 American Book Award, and a 2010 Latino Books Into Movies Award. Her second novel, *Dancing with Butterflies,* received a 2010 International Latino Book Award. Her memoir, *The Distance Between Us,* will be published in 2012 by Atria Books. Visit her at www.reynagrande.com.

STEPHANIE ELIZONDO GRIEST has mingled with the Russian Mafia, polished Chinese propaganda, and belly danced with Cuban rumba queens. These adventures inspired her award-winning memoirs *Around the Bloc: My Life in Moscow, Beijing, and Havana; Mexican Enough: My Life Between the Borderlines;* and the guidebook *100 Places Every Woman Should Go.*

As a national correspondent for The Odyssey, she once drove 45,000 miles across America in a Honda hatchback named Bertha. She has won a Hodder Fellowship to Princeton, a Richard Margolis Award for Social Justice Reporting, and a Lowell Thomas Travel Journalism Gold Prize. Visit her website at www.mexicanenough.com.

MICHELLE HERRERA MULLIGAN is the editor in chief of *Cosmopolitan for Latinas*. She edited and contributed to *Juicy Mangos*, the first-ever literary collection of Latina erotica in English, which Pulitzer Prize–winning author Oscar Hijuelos called "not only a tantalizing read, but a deeply rewarding one as well." In 2004, she coedited *Border-Line Personalities*, a collection of essays on culture clash and the contemporary American Latina experience. In 2006 she received an Outstanding Contributions to Hispanic Studies Award. Michelle has contributed to Martha Stewart's *Whole Living*, *Time* International, *Woman's Day*, *Latina*, *House & Garden*, and *Publishers Weekly*, among others. She lives in New York and is currently at work on her first novel. Visit her at www.michelleherreramulligan.com.

ADRIANA V. LÓPEZ is the founding editor of *Críticas* magazine and edited the story collections *Barcelona Noir* and *Fifteen Candles*. López's journalism has appeared in the *New York Times* and the *Washington Post*, and her essays and fiction have been published in anthologies such as *Border-Line Personalities*, *Coloniʒe This!*, and *Juicy Mangos*. She is also the translator of various works in the Spanish language, most recently *Waiting for Robert Capa* by Susana Fortes. Her short memoir *El oso y el madroño* was published in Latin America in 2012. A member of PEN America, López divides her time between New York and Madrid.

LORRAINE LÓPEZ's first book, *Soy la Avon Lady,* won the inaugural Miguel Marmól Prize. Her novel *Call Me Henri* was awarded the Paterson Prize, and her novel *The Gifted Gabaldón Sisters* was a 2008 Borders/Las Comadres Selection. López's short story collection *Homicide Survivors Picnic* was a 2010 Finalist for the PEN/Faulkner Prize. She edited a collection of essays titled *An Angle of Vision.* Her novel *The Realm of Hungry Spirits* was released in 2011. She has coedited, with Blas Falconer, *The Other Latin@.* She teaches fiction writing at Vanderbilt University.

DAISY MARTÍNEZ is the author of the cookbooks *Daisy Cooks! Latin Flavors That Will Rock Your World,* which was an IACP nominee and winner of the Best Latino Cuisine Cookbook in the World by the Gourmand World Cookbook Awards; *Daisy: Morning, Noon and Night;* and *Daisy's Holiday Cooking: Delicious Latin Recipes for Effortless Entertaining.* In 2005 she launched the cooking program *Daisy Cooks!* on PBS. As Daisy's star ascended she met the iconic Rachael Ray and this chance meeting led to Ray's production company, Watch Entertainment, producing *Viva Daisy!,* which debuted on the Food Network in 2009. Daisy's newest show continues her focus on celebrating life and family through food, while demonstrating her knowledge of the broad spectrum of Latin cuisine. In addition to her TV show, Daisy is also a regular columnist for *Every*

Day with Rachael Ray. A dedicated mother of four fantastic children, Daisy and her family reside in Brooklyn, New York.

ANA NOGALES, PhD, is a clinical psychologist, founder of Nogales Psychological Counseling, Inc., and clinical director of the nonprofit organization Casa de la Familia, which she established for victims of rape, sexual assault, child sexual and physical abuse, human trafficking, and domestic violence. She recently launched her magazine *Doctora Ana: Salud, Psicología & Vida.* She is the author of four books: *Latina Power: Using Your 7 Strengths to Say No to Abusive Relationships, Parents Who Cheat: How Children and Adults Are Affected When Their Parents Are Unfaithful, Latina Power! Using Your 7 Strengths to Create the Success You Deserve,* and *Dr. Ana Nogales' Book of Love, Sex, and Relationships.* Dr. Nogales is also a well-known television and radio psychologist as well as a writer for PsychologyToday.com and other blogs and periodicals. Visit her at www.ananogales.com.

SOFIA QUINTERO was born to and raised by a working-class Puerto Rican and Dominican family in the Bronx. After graduating from Columbia University and having a first career in public policy, she has published five novels and counting, including her award-winning Young Adult debut, *Efrain's Secret.* She cofounded the nonprofit Chica Luna Productions, which earned a Union Square Award for its work in cultivating the next generation of women-of-color filmmakers. Sofia is also the producer and creator of the web series and social network HomeGirl.TV and is presently a member of the inaugural class of the TV Writers Studio at Long Island University. When not producing *San-*

gria Street with Elisha Miranda, the self-professed Ivy League homegirl is adapting her novel *Burn* (written as Black Artemis) as a television series. Visit her at www.sofiaquintero.com.

TERESA RODRÍGUEZ is coanchor of Univision's prime-time award-winning weekly newsmagazine, *Aquí y Ahora* (Here and Now), and has received eleven Emmy awards for her outstanding work on television specials, investigative reports, and features. Her ten-year investigative report on the terrifying rapes and murders of more than 450 Mexican women in Ciudad Juárez, Mexico, was published by Atria Books in both Spanish and English, under the title *The Daughters of Juárez: A True Story of Serial Murder South of the Border,* and quickly rose to the bestseller lists. Visit her at www.teresarodriguez.tv.

ESMERALDA SANTIAGO is the author of three memoirs: *When I Was Puerto Rican, Almost a Woman,* and *The Turkish Lover,* and of the novels *América's Dream* and *Conquistadora.* Santiago was the original spokesperson for Las Comadres and Friends National Latino Book Club. Visit her at www.esmeraldasantiago.com.

FABIOLA SANTIAGO, a prize-winning journalist at the *Miami Herald* and its Metro columnist, is the author of the novel *Reclaiming Paris.* Set to the backdrop of Miami's Cuban culture and history, it's the story of a woman who switches perfumes whenever she changes lovers along her journey to reconcile the loss of family and country. Published by Simon & Schuster's Atria Books in two languages (*Siempre París* in Spanish), and chosen for a Mariposa Award as Best First Book at the International Latino Book Awards, the novel is a best-seller in Norway, where it was translated and retitled *Habanita*. Read more at www.reclaimingparis.com and her website, www.fabiolasantiago.com.

LUIS ALBERTO URREA, 2005 Pulitzer Prize finalist for non-fiction and member of the Latino Literature Hall of Fame, is a prolific and acclaimed writer who uses his dual-culture life experiences to explore greater themes of love, loss, and triumph. Born in Tijuana, Mexico, to a Mexican father and an American mother, Urrea has published extensively in all the major genres. The critically acclaimed and bestselling author of fourteen books, Urrea has won numerous awards for his poetry, fiction, and essays. *The Devil's Highway,* his 2004 nonfiction account of a group of Mexican immigrants lost in the Arizona desert, won the Lannan Literary Award and was a finalist for the Pulitzer Prize and the Pacific Rim Kiriyama Prize. Urrea attended the University of California at San Diego, earning an undergraduate degree in writing, and did his graduate studies at the University of Colorado–Boulder.

THE HISTORY OF LAS COMADRES PARA LAS AMERICAS

W hat has become an international organization of close to 15,000 women sprouted from an informal gathering of Latina professionals in April of 2000. Elizabeth García and Veronica Rivera hosted the first Las Comadres gathering in Austin, Texas, which I was fortunate to be a part of. In my adult years away from family and friends, my roots slipped away, and I was dangerously close to losing my identity. I realized that I did not want this to happen. This was why I wanted to build an organization that could feel like a home for women who, like me, wanted to connect with other like-minded Latinas. As the national and international founder of Las Comadres Para Las Americas®, I have worked for twelve years to build a multigenerational, multiracial sisterhood where Latinas can learn about and celebrate their culture while sharing professional, educational, and social connections. Our *comadrazos*®, held in different cities across the country, are open to anyone who is looking to build community. And when we can't gather face to face, we can stay abreast of local opportunities and activities through our daily email service.

My bloodline is Mexico-Americano, and I was born and raised in the U.S. as a fourth-generation Tejana. Though I spoke Spanish as a child, English became my dominant language once I entered school, since my friends were mostly non-Latino. This was not by choice. But since I did not know my history, it was very hard to feel grounded. I thought that this feeling was unique, but soon found out that many U.S. Latinos felt this desire for community and a proximity to our Latino culture as a way to preserve and celebrate who we are and where we came from. As a young woman, I also thought I wanted a large family, but after the birth of my twins, whom I love so very much, I decided that I did not! Kids are a lot of work and a huge responsibility. But I still wanted a community. After being born into a family that would eventually produce ten siblings, upon my release from the hospital I was placed into the loving arms of my aunt and uncle who raised me. I owe them my success. However, I strongly sense that being an only child until the age of ten, when my cousin David was adopted into the family, fed my overwhelming need for others.

As successful attorneys, neither Elizabeth nor Veronica had the time to devote to the upkeep of a loosely knit group, which at that time required paper, typewriters, and postage to keep everyone connected between comadrazos. I saw the potential to expand, and applied my love of technology and computer experience to transform Las Comadres into the international organization it is today. Prior to that time I had been struggling to recruit members. But once an article was published in an Austin newspaper about our "culture club," close to five hundred Latinas reached out to me to say: *I am also looking to connect with other Latinas, and I am so glad I found this group.* Then their mothers, sisters, cousins, friends, and extended families started writing or calling to ask about starting Las Comadres in their city.

I believe that the convergence of the following three elements made it possible to expand beyond our wildest dreams: the expanding awareness and use of the Internet by potential comadres; the availability of the expertise required to set up and maintain the technological systems to keep the project viable; and the personal element: time and willingness to invest to make it succeed (i.e., my passion for this organization and my husband's technical and financial support, as it began to consume our lives!).

As I began to connect Latinas in my immediate surroundings, they often left saying that what happened in those gatherings "filled their souls" until the next meeting. When I started traveling to other cities to begin comadres groups, I met numerous women who told me they had the same idea a long time ago. They had not started such a network because it really is a lot of work to keep a group together and grow it. Then I met other women who actually did form comadre groups in their communities. One of those groups had been in existence for forty years. The majority of the groups were small, and wanted to maintain the intimate connection between original members, but were interested in joining our larger network to benefit from what we could offer.

Though we're mostly English-based, meeting with others who relate to and appreciate phrases, jokes, and songs in Spanish serves to make instant connections in a way that doesn't happen with others in mainstream society. For example, we can be strangers, but if a reference is made to something about *chanclas*, similar images and memories are conjured up for us all. I believe this is what keeps us coming back to the comadrazos. We can count on these experiences to connect us to our people, our language, our laughter, our roots.

As many of you are aware, during the fifties and sixties, Mexican heritage was not positively acknowledged or portrayed in our schools, even at the university level. Consequently, I had little exposure to the history or writings of Mexican Americans. Through Las Comadres, I became acutely aware of what would become known as American Latino literature. The more I read, the more I learned about the many aspects of Latino cultures, and I became committed to spreading the word. In 2006 we started a Latina author teleconference series and in 2008 the book club was born. Las Comadres and the Association of American Publishers partnered to create the Las Comadres and Friends National Latino Book Club and Teleconference Series. Each month the book club selects a book written by a Latino author that has been published in that year. The clubs read the book and gather to discuss it, and at the end of the month all members can phone in to listen to my conversation with the author during a live teleconference. Today, I am grateful that there are now so many of us trying to support Latino authors.

This anthology of comadre stories is only the beginning. We have so much to give, so much to learn from each other. Together, we can make the future.

—Nora de Hoyos Comstock, PhD

DAISY MARTÍNEZ'S RECIPES FROM "COOKING LESSONS"

"O.S.S.M.": Old-School Stuffed Mussels *(Daisy: Morning, Noon and Night)*

Mushroom-Plantain-Stuffed Chicken Breasts with Mango-Bacon Gravy *(Daisy's Holiday Cooking)*

Fenneled-Up Brussels Sprouts *(Daisy's Holiday Cooking)*

Banana and Dulce de Leche Strudel *(Daisy: Morning, Noon and Night)*

"O.S.S.M": Old-School Stuffed Mussels

This is a traditional tapa that you can find in just about every old-school Spanish restaurant, like El Quijote, next door to the Hotel Chelsea in Manhattan. The mussel filling is creamy and loaded with bits of ham and mushroom. The crisp-golden crust is beautiful to look at and lovely to bite into. These require some last-minute attention to crisp them up in oil, but the filling can (and should) be done hours in advance.

MAKES ABOUT 40 STUFFED MUSSELS • PREP TIME: 30 MINUTES (PLUS CHILLING) • COOK TIME: 10 MINUTES

FOR THE BÉCHAMEL
3 tablespoons unsalted butter
3 tablespoons all-purpose flour
1 cup milk

FOR THE MUSSELS
1 pound small mussels scrubbed and debearded
2 tablespoons olive oil
⅓ cup finely diced yellow onion
2 cloves garlic, minced
1 cup finely chopped white or cremini mushrooms

3 ounces sliced serrano ham or prosciutto (have it cut ⅛ inch thick), cut into tiny dice (about ⅓ cup)
2 tablespoons chopped fresh flat-leaf parsley
1 tablespoon dry sherry
Kosher or fine sea salt
1 egg
1 cup plain dry bread crumbs, plus more as needed
Canola oil, for frying

1. Make the béchamel: Melt the butter in a medium saucepan over medium-low heat. Whisk in the flour and cook until the roux is smooth and bubbly but hasn't taken on any color, about 3 minutes. Pour the milk into the roux, whisking constantly until smooth. Bring to a simmer and cook, whisking constantly, until the sauce is thickened and glossy, about 4 minutes. Remove from the heat and set aside.

2. Pour ½ inch of water into a wide skillet. Bring to a boil, add the mussels, and cover the pan. Steam, shaking the pan occasionally, just until the mussels open, 3 to 4 minutes. Drain the mussels and discard the cooking liquid. Pull the mussels out of the shells and twist each shell into 2 halves. Line up the shells on a baking sheet. Chop the mussels very coarsely, put them in a small bowl, and set aside.

3. Heat the olive oil in a small skillet over medium heat. Add the onion and garlic and cook, stirring, until the onion is softened but not browned, about 4 minutes. Add the mushrooms and cook, stirring, until any liquid they have given off is evaporated. Stir in the ham and parsley and cook for 1 minute. Pour the sherry into the pan and cook until it is evaporated. Scrape the onion mixture into the bowl with the mussels and season lightly with salt. Stir in 2 tablespoons of the béchamel sauce. The filling can be made up to a day in advance. Cover it and the remaining béchamel well and refrigerate.

4. Fill as many of the mussel shells as you can with the filling, making sure the filling goes from one end of the shell to the other and mounding it very slightly. Using the remaining béchamel and working with a small spoon, coat the filling in

each shell with an even layer of béchamel just thick enough to completely mask the filling. Chill the mussels for at least 15 minutes, or up to a few hours, to firm up the béchamel.

5. Coat the mussels: Beat the egg well in a shallow bowl. Spread the bread crumbs on a plate. Holding each shell by the edges, dip only the béchamel-coated stuffing into the beaten egg, hold the mussel over the egg for a second or two to get rid of the excess, and then dip the eggy part into the bread crumbs to coat the filling completely. Return the mussels to the baking sheet, crumb side up, as you go. Once the mussels are breaded, they should be cooked within 30 minutes.

6. Heat ¾ inch of vegetable oil in a wide heavy skillet over medium heat until the tip of the handle of a wooden spoon dipped into the oil gives off a steady stream of bubbles (about 350°F). Add only as many of the mussels, crumb side down, to the oil as will fit comfortably, and fry until the crumbs are golden brown and the filling is warmed through, about 4 minutes. If the crumbs start to brown much before that, turn down the heat and wait a few minutes before frying the rest. Drain briefly on paper towels and fry the remaining mussels. Serve hot.

Mushroom-Plantain-Stuffed Chicken Breasts with Mango-Bacon Gravy

MAKES 6 SERVINGS

For Thanksgiving, turkey is the bird of choice. If you're not wild about turkey, or you think your group is too small to fuss with one, or if you're just plain turkeyed out, it may be time to turn your attention to another bird altogether—in this case breast of chicken stuffed with sizzled mushrooms and sweet plantains and sauced with a smoky-sweet pan gravy.

I'll tell you up front that this dish requires some time in the kitchen. I'll also tell you that that time can be spread out over 3 days prior to the dinner. Come showtime, you'll look like a pro as you calmly pull together all your prepared items for a truly special main course. (Not to mention that the gravy gets *better* after a couple of days.)

Whether you're preparing the stuffed chicken breasts or a simpler, pan-roasted version, you really need skin-on chicken for this—the crispness of the skin after it's been pan-seared is lovely with the silky gravy and the chunky-chewy plantain mash.

FOR THE STUFFED
CHICKEN BREASTS:
Mushroom Picadillo
Ripe Plantain Mash
Three 3½-pound chickens
   (preferably free-range and/
   or organic)
Kosher or fine sea salt and
   freshly ground pepper

FOR THE MANGO-BACON
GRAVY:
12 ounces slab bacon, rind
   removed, cut into ½-inch
   cubes (about 2 cups)
1 large onion, halved, then cut
   into thick slices
2 medium carrots, peeled and
   coarsely chopped

4 stalks celery, trimmed and
   coarsely chopped
3 cloves garlic, coarsely
   chopped
¼ cup all-purpose flour
6 cups homemade or store-
   bought chicken broth
2 sprigs fresh thyme
1 bay leaf
1 teaspoon black peppercorns
1½ cups mango nectar (see
   Note)
2 tablespoons white wine
   vinegar
   _____
2 tablespoons olive oil
Fenneled-Up Brussels Sprouts
   for serving

1. Make the *picadillo* and the plantain mash. The *picadillo* can be made up to 3 days in advance and the plantains can be made up to 1 day in advance.

PREPARE AND CUT UP THE CHICKENS:

2. Rinse the giblets and necks and set them all, except for the livers, aside for the gravy. Use the livers for another dish or discard them.

3. For each chicken, feel along the center of the chicken breast to

find the thin bone that separates the two breast halves. With a thin-bladed knife, cut along one side of this bone and down to the rib bones. Pull the breast meat away from the center bone—so you can get a better look at what you're doing—and using the tip of the knife, start to separate the breast meat from the rib bones. Keep going like this, following the curve of the rib bones, until you reach the joint where the wing connects to the breastbone. Cut through the skin along the backbone—but not through the skin that connects the breast to the thigh (you'll get to that in a minute). When you reach the point where the wing bone connects to the breastbone, bend the wing behind the chicken to give yourself a very clear view of the joint. Cut through the joint to separate the wing from the breastbone. You now have a skin-on boneless breast (with the wing attached) that is still attached to the thigh by the skin. Slip your fingertip under the skin of the thigh to separate the skin from the meat. Pull back the skin from the leg, leaving the skin attached to the breast. Cut off as much of the skin from the thigh as you can, being sure to leave that skin attached to the skin that covers the breast. Cut off the wing tip and middle joint of the wing, leaving the first joint of the wing attached to the breast. (This is known as a Frenched chicken breast.) You will now have a boneless chicken breast with a fair amount of extra skin (from the thigh) attached along one edge and the first wing joint attached to the other end. Trim any pieces of fat or cartilage from the breast and repeat with the other breast half. When you've finished removing the two breasts, remove the legs by bending them backward to expose the joints that connect the legs to the backbone. Cut through the skin, meat,

and those joints to remove the legs. Set the legs and trimmed
wing pieces aside for another use. Trim all the fat and skin
from the breastbones and backbones of the 3 chickens and,
with a heavy knife or a cleaver, whack the bones into manage-
able pieces. Set the bones aside for the gravy.

BUTTERFLY AND STUFF THE CHICKEN BREASTS:

4. To butterfly the chicken, start at the wider, thicker long side
of each breast and make a horizontal cut almost all the way
through the breast, stopping just before cutting through the
thin side of the breast. Season both sides of the breasts with
salt and pepper.

5. Take ¼ cup of the plantain mash and shape it into a more or
less even roll about 2 inches long. Repeat to make 5 more
rolls and set them aside. Open up one of the butterflied
chicken breasts with one of the long sides closest to you.
Spread ¼ cup of the mushroom *picadillo* over the surface of
the meat, leaving about a ½-inch border all the way around.
Place one of the plantain rolls along the edge of the chicken
breast closest to you. Roll up the chicken breast, tucking in
the ends as you go, to make a neat, compact little bundle with
the wing joint protruding from one end. There will be a little
skin left on the far side—smooth that into place to cover up
the seam and to cover up as much of the breast meat as possible and make an even neater bundle. With the seam side
down, tie the stuffed breast at 1-inch intervals with kitchen
twine. Do the same with the rest of the breasts, mushroom
picadillo, and plantain rolls. Pat the stuffed breasts dry with
paper towels. The chickens can be boned and seasoned up to

2 days before cooking them, and the breasts can be stuffed up to several hours before. Keep them refrigerated in a covered container.

6. Put the bacon cubes in a wide braising pan or casserole and pour in ¼ cup water. Set over high heat and cook until the water is almost evaporated, then reduce the heat to medium low. *(Starting the bacon with a little water helps pull some of the fat out of the bacon. By the time the water has evaporated, the bacon will be sizzling gently in its own fat.)* Cook until the bacon is lightly browned and the bottom of the pan is shiny with golden bits stuck to it, about 6 minutes. Add the onion, carrots, celery, and garlic and cook, stirring often so the vegetables do not stick and brown, until the onion is softened but not brown, about 10 minutes.

7. Add the reserved chicken bones and giblets and cook, stirring often, until the bones start to brown and the onion is well browned, about 10 minutes. Poke around the bottom of the pan as you stir to make sure the bones and vegetables aren't sticking and burning as they cook. Sprinkle the flour over the bones and vegetables and stir until you can't see any traces of white. Pour in the broth and add the thyme, bay leaf, and peppercorns. Bring to a boil, stirring up the little browned bits that have stuck to the pan. Adjust the heat so the sauce is simmering and stir in the mango nectar and the vinegar. Cook until the sauce is slightly thickened, smooth, and a rich brown, about 45 minutes. Stir occasionally to prevent sticking, especially in the corners of the pan. Strain the gravy through a

very fine sieve. The gravy can be held at room temperature for up to 2 hours or refrigerated for up to 3 days. In either case, reheat the gravy over low heat, adding water a spoonful at a time to return it to its original thickness.

COOK THE STUFFED CHICKEN BREASTS AND ASSEMBLE THE PLATES:

8. About 35 minutes before you're ready to serve the chicken, preheat the oven to 400°F. When it reaches that temperature, heat the 2 tablespoons olive oil in a large, heavy, ovenproof nonstick skillet over medium-high heat. Be sure the chicken breasts are dry and slide them carefully into the oil. Cook, turning as necessary, until they're beautifully browned on all sides, about 10 minutes. Pop the whole pan into the oven and cook until the chicken is cooked through and the filling is warmed, about 20 minutes. *(The best way to check is to use an instant-read thermometer. The temperature at the very center of the stuffing should reach 150°F.)*

9. Let the chicken breasts rest for about 5 minutes. Meanwhile, cook the prepared Brussels sprouts and make sure the gravy is hot.

10. To serve: Snip the twine off the chicken breasts. Slice the breasts on the diagonal into 4 or 5 slices each. Arrange the slices overlapping along one side of each plate. Spoon some Brussels sprouts onto the other side of the plate. Ladle enough gravy over the sliced chicken to nap it and form a little pool on the plate. Serve immediately.

Note: Mango nectar is a pulpy juice extracted from fresh mangoes. It is available fresh in cartons in some Latin markets and health food stores or in bottles, cartons, or cans in many supermarkets.

Mushroom *Picadillo*

To the French, this is known as *duxelles*—a simple mixture of sautéed mushrooms and shallots. In my world, it reminds me of *picadillo,* the well-seasoned ground beef (or pork) dish that is eaten on its own or used as a filling for turnovers, vegetables, or croquettes.

If you don't mind the chopping, triple the recipe (cooking each batch separately), freeze two-thirds, and you'll be all set for a batch of Mushroom Croquettes and a whole lot more: Use these mushrooms to liven up a pot of soup or stew or as an *empanadita* filling, or stir a few spoonfuls into your next pan of simple white rice.

One 14-ounce package white
    mushrooms
2 tablespoons olive oil
2 small shallots, finely chopped

Kosher or fine sea salt and
    freshly ground pepper
Lemon juice

1. Wipe the mushroom caps clean with a damp paper towel. Cut the caps in half and then slice them thin. Chop them fine by rocking your knife back and forth over them, a little mound at a time. You'll have about 8 cups. *(This is a labor of love. You may be tempted to chop the mushrooms in a food processor, but that would make them mushy, and you wouldn't end up with the nicely browned, pebbly texture of hand-chopped mushrooms.)*

2. Heat the oil in a large skillet over medium-high heat. Add the shallots and cook, stirring, until they're softened, about 3 minutes. Add the mushrooms and stir until they give up enough liquid to coat the bottom of the pan. Reduce the heat to medium-low and cook until all the liquid has evaporated and the tiny pieces of mushroom are separate, almost fluffy. Season with salt and pepper and enough lemon juice to give it a lively zing. The *picadillo* will keep in the refrigerator for up to 4 days or up to 2 months in the freezer.

Ripe Plantain Mash

(NOT QUITE *MOFONGO*)

MAKES ABOUT 4 CUPS

Maybe I should start by explaining what *mofongo* is before I tell you why this isn't quite it. *Mofongo* starts with green (i.e., unripe, starchy) plantains that are cooked and then mashed with garlic, pork cracklings, and the fat rendered from making the cracklings, to a coarse and crunchy mash. Diet food, it isn't—delicious, it is.

When I first made this simple mixture of ripened plantains as a filling for the chicken breasts, I boiled the plantains until fully tender and mashed them until smooth. Then I tried a version with slightly-less-than-tender plantains mashed coarsely, like *mofongo*, and found I liked that texture much better.

If your bird is a whole turkey, serve this as an unexpected side dish, along with the usual yams and cranberry sauce. Or whip up a batch of this not-quite-*mofongo* and serve alongside fried eggs, chorizo, and pickled onion for breakfast on a chilly autumn morning.

3 medium plantains (see Note),   *2 tablespoons unsalted butter*
    peeled and cut into 3 pieces each   *Freshly ground pepper*
Kosher or fine sea salt

1. Put the plantains in a medium saucepan and add enough water to cover by a couple of inches. Add a rounded teaspoon of salt and bring to a boil over high heat. Adjust the

heat so the water is simmering. Cook until you can pierce the plantains easily with a paring knife, but there is still some texture, about 6 minutes.

2. Drain the plantains and let them air-dry for a few minutes. Put them in a food processor along with the butter and 2 tablespoons water. Process, using very quick on-off pulses, just until the smaller pieces of plantain are starting to become smooth. The texture should be very coarse and you should still be able to see pieces of plantain in the mash. Scrape into a bowl and season to taste with salt and pepper. Serve hot.

Note: The skin of the plantains should be mostly black with some speckling of yellow. The flesh should have some give when you press it with your thumb.

Fenneled-Up Brussels Sprouts

❖

We all know that overcooking Brussels sprouts is a pretty mean thing to do to them. I'm making a 180-degree turn and suggesting that you cook your sprouts for a matter of minutes. Slicing them thin makes this possible. Teaming the sprouts up with fennel seeds makes them delicious.

Two 10-ounce containers or 1¼ pounds loose Brussels sprouts

2 tablespoons olive oil

1 teaspoon fennel seeds

Kosher or fine sea salt and freshly ground pepper

1. Trim the little stalk off the end of each sprout. Cut the sprouts in half, then cut the halves—flat side down, so they stay steady—into thin (about ⅛-inch) shreds. You will have about 7 cups shredded sprouts. The sprouts may be shredded up to several hours before cooking them.

2. Heat the oil in a large, heavy skillet over medium-high heat. Add the fennel seeds and cook just until they smell wonderful and are sizzling. Stir in the sprouts and cook, tossing and stirring the sprouts, until they are wilted down, bright green, and softened, about 4 minutes. Pull the pan from the heat and season with salt and pepper to taste. Serve hot.

Banana and
Dulce de Leche Strudel

My friend Paula's sister, Maria *Grande* (to distinguish her from her gorgeous daughter, Maria *Chiquita*), made arrangements for us to eat at a restaurant called Social Paraiso in Buenos Aires. The dessert was called *delicia tibia de banana*, and it resembled a phyllo "cigar" with a warm banana center and a drizzle of dulce de leche.

MAKES 12 SERVINGS • PREP TIME: 30 MINUTES
• COOK TIME: 30 MINUTES

6 ripe bananas

Juice of 1 lemon

1¼ cups sugar

*½ cup plus 2 tablespoons heavy
cream*

4 tablespoons unsalted butter

¼ teaspoon ground cinnamon

1 cup coarsely chopped pecans

16 sheets phyllo dough

*6 tablespoons unsalted butter,
melted*

*1 cup finely crumbled dry-
textured almond cookies
(such as Stella D'oro),
amaretti, or anise toasts*

1. Slice the bananas lengthwise into quarters, then cut them crosswise into ½-inch-or-so pieces. Toss them in a bowl with the lemon juice and set aside.

2. Using the sugar and ¼ cup water, make a caramel. As soon as the caramel is done, remove the pan from the heat and (carefully!) pour the cream into the pan. It will bubble up,

then die down. As soon as it is safe, whisk the caramel until smooth and creamy. Return the skillet to low heat and whisk in the butter 1 tablespoon at a time. Whisk in the cinnamon and set aside to cool briefly.

3. Add the caramel and pecans to the bananas and stir well but gently. Set aside.

4. Preheat the oven to 375°F. Line a baking sheet with parchment paper.

5. Lay the phyllo sheets out on a work surface and cover them with a damp kitchen towel. Remove 2 sheets of phyllo, set them on a dry clean towel, and brush the top sheet with melted butter. Sprinkle about 2 tablespoons of the crumbled cookies over the butter. Repeat 3 more times to make 4 layers of phyllo, butter, and cookies. Spoon half of the banana mixture over the center of the top sheet of phyllo, leaving at least 1 inch on both of the short ends and about 2 inches on the long sides. Using the towel, fold the long sides of the phyllo over the filling, then pinch the ends together to seal. Flip the log onto the prepared baking sheet and tuck the ends under the log. Repeat the process to make another strudel.

6. Brush the strudels with butter and bake until golden and crispy on top, 25 to 30 minutes. Serve warm or at room temperature, cut crosswise into slices.

Count *on* Me
Las Comadres Para Las Americas
A Readers Club Guide

INTRODUCTION

Las Comadres Para Las Americas is an international organization that has been bringing together thousands of Latinas across
the Unites States for more than twenty-five years to count on,
lean on, help, and advise one another. In this moving collection
of twelve new personal essays, accomplished authors from the
organization share their own stories of how a comadre influ-
enced their lives. These are tales of how these sisterly bonds can
enrich our lives in every possible way.

TOPICS AND QUESTIONS FOR DISCUSSION

1. Discuss the concept of the comadre, or co-mother. How
   does the term itself convey a relationship stronger and more
   complex than friendship? How does each of the essays in
   this collection shed light on the idea of the comadre? Do
   you have your own comadres?

2. In "Las Comais," Esmeralda Santiago discusses how the
   women of her Puerto Rican community raised each other's
   children, while the men worked away from the barrio all
   day. How did the men's absence make the women's bond

stronger? How did Esmeralda's mother's comadres become linked to her own survival?

3. How is watching over a dead friend's book (from "Every Day of Her Life") similar to being an adoptive parent? How does the act of writing bring together Carolina and Leila, as well as so many of the other women in this collection? How does being a writer inform their friendship?

4. "I can't help but view marriage as a loss. My loss," writes Stephanie Elizondo Griest in "Road Sisters." (p. 66) She also states: "Babies are worse than husbands." (p. 67) Have you ever "lost" a friend in such a manner? Are there ways to keep a friendship even as she (or you) starts a family?

5. In "Crocodiles and Plovers," Lorraine López discusses her relationship with an inspiring mentor. Have you ever had such a relationship? Can a mentor/mentee friendship ever be truly equal? How?

6. Fabiola Santiago writes of a childhood friend she left behind in "Letters from Cuba." Do you have any childhood friends who are still a strong presence in your life? Do you have much in common with them in your adult life? Is there a special bond between two people who have grown up in similar environments?

7. In "Casa Amiga," Teresa Rodríguez memorializes a woman who stood up for women's civil rights in a dangerous area of Mexico where machismo ruled. How did Esther Chávez Cano become a comadre both to the woman who wrote about her as well as to the women she helped to rescue? Even though she and Esther weren't close in every sense of the word, Teresa still felt a close connection to her. How

does the idea of comadre-ship in this story differ from that of friendship?

8. Sofia Quintero lays out many rules for friendship—from the serious to the humorous—in "The Miranda Manual." What are some lessons about friendship that you have learned over the years? Share some of your own rules with your book group.

9. Many of the essays in this collection detail the hardships of emigration; how moving to the Unites States made the writers feel unmoored. In "My Teacher, My Friend," Reyna Grande feels alone and oppressed by her abusive father until she meets her mentor, Diana. Are there ways in which the bonds of friendship are stronger than family? How does Reyna's essay illustrate this concept?

10. Are there certain foods that remind you of a friend or a loved one? How does the act of cooking bring the women in "Cooking Lessons" together? Is there an activity that you and your friends do together that brings you closer?

11. In "Anarchy Chicks," Michelle Herrera Mulligan writes of a childhood friendship that remains a constant even as she grows up and her identity goes through a variety of changes. How does her appreciation for her culture change as she gets older? Do you find that as an adult you are more likely to value your heritage? Why or why not?

12. In "Heart to Heart Connection," Ana Nogales poses the question, "Were the immigrant experiences of those from other Latin American countries that different from my own?" (p. 194) She came to the conclusion that yes, they were. Do you agree? How did class and religion factor into

Ana's childhood isolation, and how did nuances in Latin culture ultimately prove just as baffling? In what ways can Latinas of all backgrounds unite?

13. How does the inclusion of a man, Luis Alberto Urrea, change your view of what a comadre can be? Do you agree with Luis when he writes: "It is possible for men and women to be deep friends, I think. It is necessary." (p. 209) Have you had deep and meaningful friendships with members of the opposite sex? Can a man be an honorary comadre?

ENHANCE YOUR BOOK CLUB

1. In her introduction to the collection, Nora de Hoyos Comstock mentions a young Latina, recently graduated from college, who had never read a book by a Latina author before. Have you? Who are your favorites? If you are not part of Las Comadres and Friends National Latino Book Club, which selects its entire reading list at the beginning of each year, choose another Latina author for your next book club discussion.

2. Pretend that you have been asked to contribute to *Count on Me* and write a short essay or story of your own about a comadre. Share your story with your book group members.

3. Assign each member of your book group a recipe from "Cooking Lessons" to prepare for a group dinner. Or buy all the ingredients and gather together to cook dinner as a group.